Privileged Anonymity
The Writings of Madame de Lafayette

LEGENDA

European Humanities Research Centre
Research Monographs in French Studies

Privileged Anonymity
The Writings of Madame de Lafayette

❖

ANNE GREEN

European Humanities Research Centre
Research Monographs in French Studies 1
1996

Published for the Society for French Studies by the
European Humanities Research Centre
of the University of Oxford
37a St Giles'
Oxford OX1 3LD

LEGENDA is the publications imprint of the
European Humanities Research Centre

ISBN 1 900755 00 9

First published 1996

All rights reserved. No part of this publication may be reproduced or disseminated or transmitted in any form or by any means, electronic, mechanical, photocopying, recording or otherwise, or stored in any retrieval system, or otherwise used in any manner whatsoever without the express permission of the copyright owner

British Library Cataloguing in Publication Data
A CIP catalogue record for this book is available from the British Library

© European Humanities Research Centre of the University of Oxford 1996

LEGENDA series designed by Cox Design Partnership, Witney, Oxon
Printed in Great Britain by Remous Ltd.,
Milborne Port, Sherborne, Dorset

CONTENTS

1	Introduction	1
2	The *Histoire de Madame* and the *Mémoires de la cour de France*	9
3	*La Comtesse de Tende*	31
4	*La Princesse de Montpensier*	41
5	*Zaïde*	50
6	*La Princesse de Clèves*	64
7	Conclusion	81
	Bibliography	85
	Index	91

CHAPTER 1

Introduction

During Madame de Lafayette's lifetime (1634–93) only one of her writings—a brief portrait of her friend Madame de Sévigné—was published under her name. The rest of her work appeared anonymously or pseudonymously, or else was not published until after her death.[1] The reasons why an author may wish to remain anonymous are often highly complex, as Adrien Baillet, a contemporary of Madame de Lafayette, well understood when he analysed fourteen possible motives for choosing anonymity, ranging from the intention to defraud to the embarrassment of having a ludicrous name, and including shame at publishing a work unworthy of the author's social status, disdain for transitory glory, the wish to avoid adverse criticism, and simple fun—'le mouvement d'une pure gayeté de cœur'.[2] Although some of these motives can clearly be ruled out in the case of Madame de Lafayette, it is more difficult to know with certainty which factors were influential in her decision. Yet the question needs to be explored, for the problems surrounding the issue of anonymity are crucial to an understanding of her work.

It is clear that the withholding of Madame de Lafayette's name

---

[1] *Zaïde* was published under the signature of Madame de Lafayette's probable collaborator, Jean de Segrais, and *La Princesse de Montpensier* and *La Princesse de Clèves* both appeared anonymously during her lifetime. Within forty years of her death three new works had been published under her name: the *Histoire de Madame Henriette d'Angleterre* (1720), *La Comtesse de Tende* (1724) and the *Mémoires de la cour de France pour les années 1688 et 1689* (1731). *Zaïde* and *La Princesse de Clèves* first appeared under her name in 1780 and *La Princesse de Montpensier* in 1804. More dubious attributions have continued to be made to her. On the other hand, Geneviève Mouligneau has attempted to cast serious doubt on Madame de Lafayette's status, arguing in *Madame de Lafayette, romancière?* (Brussels: Editions de l'Université de Bruxelles, 1980) that the principal authors of the works now attributed to her were La Rochefoucauld, Huet and, in particular, Segrais.

[2] *Auteurs déguisez sous des noms étrangers; empruntez, supposez, feints à plaisir, chiffrez, renversez, retournez, ou changez d'une langue en une autre* (Paris: Dezallier, 1690), Part II, chs. i–iv.

from the title-pages of her books was a deliberate decision. Her famous letter to Ménage, written after she had discovered that a manservant had taken and circulated the manuscript of *La Princesse de Montpensier*, leaves no doubt about her desire for anonymity: 'une copie de *La Princesse de Montpensier* [. . .] court le monde; mais par bonheur ce n'est pas sous mon nom. Je vous conjure, si vous en entendez parler, de faire bien comme si vous ne l'aviez jamais veue et de nier qu'elle vienne de moy si par hasard on le disoit.'[3] She was mortified to discover that her friend Huet had passed a copy of the same book to his sister and had revealed the name of its author: 'Elle croira que je suis un vray auteur de profession de donner comme cela de mes livres,' she complained. 'Je vous prie, raccommodez un peu ce que cette imaginative pourroit avoir gasté à l'opinion que je souhaite qu'elle ait de moy.'[4] And a month after the publication of *La Princesse de Clèves* she was again writing to deny rumours that she and La Rochefoucauld had written it: 'Un petit livre qui a couru il y a quinze ans et où il plut au public de me donner part, a fait qu'on m'en donne encore à *La Princesse de Clèves*. Mais je vous asseure que je n'y en ay aucune et que M. de La Rochefoucauld, à qui on l'a voulu donner aussi, y en a aussi peu que moy.'[5]

Feminist critics in particular have tended to argue that anonymous publication of women's writing is an instance of the suppression of the female voice; they claim that the opprobrium attached to women writers was an extension of codes of behaviour which inhibited women from public expression. But the view of Madame de Lafayette's anonymity as symptomatic of a social silencing of women is not entirely convincing, for the argument needs to be assessed within the context of the publishing practice of the period. Far from being a female anomaly in a world of male discourse, anonymous publication was extremely common among writers of both sexes in seventeenth-century France. In 1685, Baillet noted with disapproval that the device of anonymity had been fashionable in France for half a century.[6] Moreover, it had been so widespread in the previous century that civil and ecclesiastical authorities had repeatedly insisted that

---

[3] *Correspondance*, ed. A. Beaunier, 2 vols. (Paris: Gallimard, 1942), i. 169 (June or July 1662).
[4] *Corr.* i. 175 (to Huet, 15 Oct. 1662).
[5] *Corr.* ii. 62–3 (to Lescheraine, Madame Royale's secretary, 13 Apr. 1678).
[6] Baillet, *Jugemens des sçavans sur les principaux ouvrages des auteurs*, 5 vols. (Paris: Dezallier, 1685–6), i. 471.

publications must bear their author's name. Although these edicts applied only to political and religious works by the time that Madame de Lafayette was writing, in other areas the tradition of anonymous publication continued. The majority of novels published in France between 1600 and 1700 were unsigned.[7]

Another explanation frequently offered for Madame de Lafayette's decision to conceal her identity—and with it, her gender as a writer—is one of propriety: it was not considered seemly for women of a certain social class to display themselves in print.[8] In the much quoted words of Mademoiselle de Scudéry, who published her own early novels under her brother's name, 'dès [. . .] qu'on acquiert la réputation [. . .] d'écrire assez bien en vers ou en prose pour pouvoir faire des livres, on perd la moitié de sa noblesse si l'on en a'.[9] It is certainly true that most of the women who published their writings under their own names during the second half of the seventeenth century were of lower social status than Madame de Lafayette, and, more importantly, did not have her standing at court.[10] And it is also the case that, if it was considered demeaning to write and to publish, it was even worse to publish novels, which ranked low in the hierarchy of seventeenth-century literary genres.[11]

[7] See Maurice Lever, 'Romans en quête d'auteurs au XVIIe siècle', *Revue d'histoire littéraire de la France* 73 (1973), 7–21 (esp. 8–9).

[8] See Roger Duchêne, *Madame de Lafayette, la romancière aux cent bras* (Paris: Fayard, 1988), 200: 'Applicable aux hommes d'un certain rang, la règle de ne pas imprimer sous son nom est encore plus contraignante pour les femmes.' Cf. Charles Sorel's reference to '*La Nouvelle de la Princesse de Montpensier*, laquelle vient d'une personne de haute condition, et d'excellent esprit, qui se contente de faire de belles choses, sans que son nom soit publié' (*Bibliothèque française* (1664), edn. of 1667), cit. Maurice Laugaa, *Lectures de Madame de Lafayette* (Paris: Colin, 1971), 10.

[9] In 'L'Histoire de Sapho', cit. Nicole Aronson, *Mademoiselle de Scudéry ou le voyage au pays de Tendre* (Paris: Fayard, 1986), 43. Cf. Père René Rapin's view: 'Dans un siècle aussi éclairé et aussi critique que le nôtre, on s'humilie dès que l'on se déclare Auteur. En effet, la rigueur est si grande, qu'il n'y a point de mérite, quelque établi qui soit, qui s'en sauve . . .' (*Instructions pour l'Histoire* (Paris: Sébastier Mabre-Cramoisy, 1677), 147, cit. Marc Fumaroli, *La Diplomatie de l'esprit. De Montaigne à La Fontaine* (Paris: Hermann, 1994), 189).

[10] 'Les autoresses, assez nombreuses, de la deuxième moitié du siècle, Mme de Villedieu, Mme d'Aulnoy, Mme de Murat, Mlle de la Force, etc., étaient presque toutes des aventurières, ou alors, comme Mlle de la Roche-Guilhem, des émigrées (pour crime de protestantisme) que leur soudaine pauvreté contraignait à gagner leur pain comme elles pouvaient.' Claude Dulong, *La Vie quotidienne des femmes au grand siècle* (Paris: Hachette, 1984), 12.

[11] See Lever, 11.

A clear distinction must of course be made between work written for private circulation among an élite circle and work intended for general publication. Madame de Lafayette certainly did not want to be thought of as 'un vray auteur de profession', yet this desire is insufficient to explain her concern not to allow her literary abilities to be known. Segrais records that she did not even want it to be known that she understood Latin, 'afin de ne pas attirer sur elle la jalousie des autres Dames'.[12] According to La Rochefoucauld, she was also unhappy at the thought of others learning of her knowledge of poetry and her ability to write verse. He tried to reassure her, telling her that 'pour votre façon d'écrire en Prose, *dont il n'y a point de danger de parler*, il n'y a rien de plus naturel et de plus délicat'.[13] Such apparent modesty exceeded that which the conventions of propriety required, and yet, curiously, despite her professed desire for anonymity, Madame de Lafayette's literary talents were widely known. Many of her contemporaries commented on her prowess. One admirer writes of her in 1669 that 'Outre sa langue où elle se fait admirer, elle en sait cinq ou six autres, et a lu tout ce qu'il y a de beaux Livres en toutes ces langues. Elle écrit parfaitement bien, et n'a nul empressement de montrer ses ouvrages.'[14] In the preface to her *Histoire de Madame Henriette d'Angleterre* she herself admits that it was because of her reputation as a writer that she was chosen by Princess Henriette to record her confidences; by 1685 Baillet was referring to her in his *Jugemens des sçavans* as one of the most accomplished people in the realm, and Boileau called her the most intelligent woman in France and the best woman writer.[15] With comments such as these coming from contemporaries belonging to a range of social levels, it was clearly no secret that she wrote, and wrote well. No one seems to have suggested that her skill as a writer was inappropriate or unseemly. As we shall see, this curious contradiction between seemingly excessive reticence and the widespread respect with which her

---

[12] *Segraisiana* (1721), 102, cit. Mouligneau, 22.

[13] He went on to observe that her talent was such that she could produce in half an hour what it would take 'ceux-mesmes qui passent pour les maistres' a whole day to write. La Rochefoucauld, *Portrait de Mle*** sous le nom de Climene*, in *Recüeil des Portraits et Éloges en vers et en prose dédié à son Altesse Royalle Mademoiselle*, 643–7, cit. Mouligneau, 31.

[14] *L'Amour échapé* (Paris, 1669), iii. 6–7, cit. Alain Niderst in Madame de Lafayette, *Romans et nouvelles*, ed. E. Magne (Paris: Garnier, 1970), p. vii.

[15] Baillet, *Jugemens des sçavans sur les principaux ouvrages des auteurs*, iv. 180.

writing was regarded is symptomatic of a constant in all her work, namely the tension between self-effacement and the conquest of public esteem.

Perhaps the most striking example of these conflicting impulses comes with the publication of her best-known novel, *La Princesse de Clèves*. It has been suggested that Madame de Lafayette's name was withheld from the title-page of that work not for reasons of propriety but as part of a carefully orchestrated publicity campaign conducted by her publisher.[16] The enigma of the unknown author would clearly appeal to the same public who enjoyed trying to solve the 'énigmes' published regularly in *Le Mercure galant*, and who sent in their solutions under such elaborate pseudonyms that the editor was obliged to print a notice asking them to restrain themselves.[17] The suggestion is a persuasive one, but since Madame de Lafayette's other works were not published with the same fanfares as *La Princesse de Clèves*, and since some were not published at all during her lifetime, it is hardly a comprehensive explanation.

Joan DeJean has put forward a different hypothesis which also contradicts the notion that Madame de Lafayette's anonymity is simply a sign of self-effacement. In an astute analysis of *La Princesse de Clèves*, she sees the lack of signature, instead, as a 'carefully calculated strategy' which focuses the reader's attention on the text rather than on the author. She contends that in *La Princesse de Clèves* this strategy is an attempt 'to avoid the loss of authority that accompanies every public appropriation of fictionalized feminine desire and to create enigma from the protection of privacy, thus generating new privileges of anonymity'. Both Madame de Lafayette's choice of anonymity and the fictional Princess's renunciation of marriage and public life are seen as affirmations of the woman writer's authority.[18]

But not all Madame de Lafayette's writing can be interpreted as having such an assertive message. Her motives were neither constant nor unambiguous. Although she is flustered at the prospect of being 'found out', she is at the same time flattered at being thought the author of *La Princesse de Clèves*. Madame de Seneville reports that while La Rochefoucauld and Madame de Lafayette hotly denied

---

[16] See e.g. Laugaa, 14 ff.
[17] *Le Mercure galant*, May 1678, preface (n.p.).
[18] Joan DeJean, 'Lafayette's Ellipses: The Privileges of Anonymity', *PMLA* 99, (Oct. 1984), 884–902.

being the authors of *La Princesse de Clèves*, they nevertheless praised it to the skies.[19] As Madame de Lafayette commented to Lescheraine in a letter denying her authorship, 'je suis flattée que l'on me soupçonne et je croy que j'avoûrais le livre, si j'estois asseurée que l'autheur ne vînt jamais me le redemander. Je le trouve très agréable, bien escrit sans estre extrêmement châtié, plein de choses d'une délicatesse admirable et qu'il faut mesme relire plus d'une fois. Et surtout, ce que j'y trouve, c'est une parfaite imitation du monde de la cour et de la manière dont on y vit.'[20] By disclaiming her authorship, she can not only take delight in the book's success but add to that success by singing its praises—without loss of modesty.

Some of the clearest insights into her choice of anonymity occur, paradoxically, in the one work that she did sign—the portrait of Madame de Sévigné. This was her first publication and appeared in *La Galerie des peintures ou recueil des portraits et éloges en vers et en prose*, a collection of short word-portraits of members of the court which was presented to Mademoiselle de Montpensier in 1659. Contributors to the volume indicate their identities in a wide variety of ways: some give their real names, some give classical pseudonyms or initials, some give only an indication of their sex, some leave their piece totally unsigned. But Madame de Lafayette's contribution falls into none of these categories. It is both signed and anonymous, and its author is both female and male: 'fait par Madame la comtesse de la Fayette, sous le Nom d'un Inconnu'.[21]

Clearly, Madame de Lafayette's pose of anonymity and male impersonation here is a deliberate literary conceit, a device whose advantages are explained in the portrait itself. Its immediate effect is to free the writer from external constraints: if the author's identity is unknown, he or she cannot be blamed for what is written. Madame de Lafayette points out that conventional portraits are uniformly complimentary since authors dare not mention their subjects' shortcomings for fear of displeasing them. The anonymous male persona adopted by Madame de Lafayette explains, however, that as an *inconnu*, he can tell the unpalatable truth without risk of repercus-

---

[19] Roger de Bussy-Rabutin, *Correspondance* (Paris: Charpentier, 1858), iv. 98 (Mme de Seneville to Bussy, 25 Apr. 1678).
[20] *Corr.* ii. 63 (to Lescheraine, 13 Apr. 1678).
[21] 'Portrait de Madame la Marquise de Sévigné', in *La Galerie des peintures ou recueil des portraits et éloges en vers et en prose* (1659, 2nd edn. Paris: de Seroy, 1663), i. 200.

sions. But then, with a clever twist, the pose of anonymity becomes an ingenious conceit: free to paint Madame de Sévigné's flaws, the writer can find none. Anonymity heightens the compliment.

The anonymous male pose also appropriates additional power for the author. '[. . .] si je vous suis inconnu, vous ne m'êtes pas inconnue', Madame de Sévigné is told.[22] The subject of the portrait remains in the dark, while the hidden author assumes greater authority through his superior knowledge. 'He' poses as an unrequited lover who bemoans the fact that Madame de Sévigné's affections are directed elsewhere—at none other than Madame de Lafayette herself: 'Vous êtes naturellement tendre et passionnée', the writer tells Madame de Sévigné; 'mais à la honte de notre sexe, cette tendresse vous a été inutile, & vous l'avez renfermée dans le vôtre, en la donnant à Madame de Lafayette.'[23] By this curious sleight of hand, Madame de Lafayette teasingly purports to guarantee that she is not the author, but at the same time draws added attention to herself as author by inscribing her own name within the text and repeating the signature printed at its head. Her portrait of Madame de Sévigné stands out from the rest of the collection not only because of the inventiveness and assurance of its argument, but also because its ludic qualities both tease the readers and also focus attention on the author's identity, offering a more revealing portrait of Madame de Lafayette than of Madame de Sévigné herself.

Playful and witty, anonymous yet signed, male yet female, Madame de Lafayette's first venture into print shows a confident awareness of the positive benefits of writing without a name. By paying lip-service to the notion that women should remain modest and silent, she is in fact able to express herself more openly—a paradox which, as we shall see, the female characters of her novels frequently use to their advantage. This 'privilège d'Inconnu', as she calls it,[24] was one which she would adopt for the rest of her fiction.

But if her simultaneous absence and presence in this text is a deliberate literary contrivance, elsewhere it seems to reflect a barely expressible unease, a deep-seated preoccupation with alternative modes of being that echoes through the plots of her fiction. It is not fortuitous that words like *cacher, dissimuler, feindre* and *secret* occur so frequently in her work, or that much of her fiction turns on the delicate interplay between what is known, felt or said in private, and

---

[22] Ibid. 198–9.   [23] Ibid. 200.   [24] Ibid. 196.

what is publicly displayed. Although the bold assertiveness of the *Portrait* is missing from her subsequent novels and short stories, the Madame de Lafayette of those later works was neither a passive victim of silencing pressures, nor a heroic pioneer struggling to change the reception of women's writing. Rather, as a close reading of her later work shows, she was a writer working out conflicting attitudes to her status both as woman and as author.

CHAPTER 2

The *Histoire de Madame* and the *Mémoires de la cour de France*

Madame de Lafayette produced her two works of historical non-fiction, the *Histoire de Madame Henriette d'Angleterre* (begun in 1664) and the *Mémoires de la cour de France pour les années 1688 and 1689*, near the beginning and at the end of her literary life. These histories directly explore many of the themes and issues underlying the novels and short stories which came between. In particular, they offer fascinating insights into the complex interrelations between anonymity, reticence and creativity, between silence and speech and female power which underlie her fiction.

When the *Histoire de Madame Henriette d'Angleterre* was first translated into English at the end of the eighteenth century it was subtitled *An historical novel by the Comtesse de Lafayette*—but it is not a novel. Nor is it in any conventional sense a *Vie de Madame*, as one early manuscript version calls it. It tells us relatively little about its supposed subject, and some biographical omissions are striking. There is nothing, for example, about Henriette's perilous childhood—nothing about her mother, the Queen, fleeing from England to France only two weeks after Henriette's birth, leaving her behind in Exeter, and nothing about Henriette being disguised and smuggled to France by her governess two years later when Exeter was captured by anti-royalist troops. It is neither biography nor history nor fiction, but lies somewhere on the borderline of all three.[1]

Divided into four parts preceded by a preface, the *Histoire de Madame* begins by giving details of some of the young Louis XIV's numerous love-affairs, and describes the changing power-structure at

---

[1] For further discussion of the changing relationship between memoirs, historical narrative and fiction during this period see Fumaroli, 183–215; and Faith E. Beasley, *Revising Memory: Women's Fiction and Memoirs in Seventeenth-Century France* (New Brunswick/London: Rutgers University Press, 1990).

court when Louis unexpectedly assumed personal rule after the death of Cardinal Mazarin. The first major event to take place after the Cardinal's death is the marriage of Monsieur (Philippe d'Orléans, brother of Louis XIV) to Princess Henriette (daughter of Charles I of England), thereafter known by the courtesy title of Madame. From this point the narrative traces a series of complicated love-affairs at court and intersperses them with the odd reference to wider political events such as the downfall of Fouquet and the war in Poland. A brief flirtation develops between Madame and the King before he turns his affections to Louise de la Vallière, and Monsieur's favourite, the Comte de Guiches, falls in love with Madame. The Comtesse de Soissons, the Marquis de Vardes and Madame's intrigue-loving maid of honour, Mademoiselle de Montalais, are among those who use their knowledge of these illicit affairs to try to win power for themselves. As the *Histoire* continues, the intrigues—disguises, forged letters, secret assignations and false rumours—become ever more convoluted before fading suddenly as Henriette outmanœuvres the conspirators and concentrates instead on helping to conclude the secret Treaty of Dover between her brother, Charles II of England, and her brother-in-law, Louis XIV. The final section of the *Histoire*, written later, is a detailed account of Madame's sudden death little more than a week after her triumphant return from England.

Any history or biography naturally involves a process of sifting, selecting and shaping, just as a novel does, and in the *Histoire de Madame* we find Madame de Lafayette presenting and interpreting real events in ways that also inform her novels. Like her other writings, the text is not as straightforward as it might first appear—its disingenuously factual tone is deceptive. If we look closely at the various ways in which Madame de Lafayette has chosen and processed the facts, we discover as much about the author herself as about the Princess. In particular, we discover some vital clues to Madame de Lafayette's ambivalence about admitting her authorship.

The *Histoire de Madame* was not written for formal publication, and its preface appears to explain the genesis of the work. The version of events offered to the reader is that Princess Henriette had come to France to join her mother in exile at the convent of Sainte-Marie de Chaillot. The mother superior of this convent was Angélique de Lafayette, sister-in-law of Madame de Lafayette, and it was on her visits there that Madame de Lafayette met and became friendly with the young Princess. The affection and respect that the two women felt for one another meant that they were often together, and it was at Madame's own suggestion that Madame de Lafayette began to write down the confidences passed on to her by the Princess: 'Vous écrivez bien,' Madame told her in 1664; 'écrivez, je vous fournirai de bons Mémoires' (21).[2]

According to the preface, Henriette regularly confided details of her life and of court intrigue to Madame de Lafayette, who would set them down on paper and show the Princess her work the following morning. She describes the difficulty of trying to tell the truth and yet present it in a way that would not offend Madame. For a time the Princess was very enthusiastic about her memoirs, even writing some herself when Madame de Lafayette was absent for two days. But when Henriette began to tire of the project, Madame de Lafayette put it aside: the writing was abandoned and forgotten for several years before being taken up again in 1669. In 1670 the work was cut short by Madame's sudden death: 'La mort de cette princesse ne me laissa ni le dessein ni le goût de continuer cette Histoire' (22).

In this preface, then, Madame de Lafayette presents the *Histoire de Madame* as a simple piece of amusement written with the sole purpose of entertaining the Princess. The author portrays herself as little more than a scribe, an almost passive secretary who writes at the express wish of Madame, relinquishes her pen to her at one point, and stops writing as soon as the Princess tires of telling her story. She seems to deny that there is anything of *herself* in the work: she indicates that it was not her idea in the first place, and that much of what she writes is a virtual transcription of Madame's account.[3]

But like so many of Madame de Lafayette's statements about her writing, this picture of self-effacement cannot be taken at face value. If she wrote the *Histoire* only to please Madame, why did she include a detailed account of Madame's death?[4] And why did she return to

---

[2] References in brackets are to *Histoire de Madame Henriette d'Angleterre suivie de Mémoires de la cour de France pour les années 1688 et 1689*, ed. Gilbert Sigaux (Paris: Mercure de France, 1965).

[3] The title may be seen as a reinforcement of this effacement. Is the *Histoire de Madame* perhaps to be read not as 'the story (or history) *of* Madame' but as 'a story (or history) *by* Madame', with Madame de Lafayette's part in it reduced to that of amanuensis?

[4] Writing at the beginning of the 19th century, the novelist and moralizer Madame de Genlis took strong exception to the *Histoire*. If Madame was foolish enough to want posterity to know about her intrigues with Vardes and the Comte de Guiches, Madame de Lafayette should have refused to co-operate. Rather than

the work many years later to add an explanatory preface to what purports to be a quite private piece of documentation?[5] The answer can only be that Madame de Lafayette set greater store by it than she allows. Her suggestion that it was written solely for Madame's amusement has to be discounted.[6]

In this work, her reticence is more than balanced by self-revelation. For once, she admits in the text that she is indeed the author, and she even provides a deceptively modest self-portrait (written in the third person).[7] Living on the fringes of a court where the slightest mark of royal favour was noted and envied, Madame de Lafayette must have derived considerable prestige from Madame's friendship and confidences.[8] So it is not surprising that on this occasion Madame de Lafayette was willing not only to acknowledge her authorship but to draw particular attention to her name. She begins the work with the story of Louis XIII's love and esteem for her sister-in-law, Angélique de Lafayette; she notes that Angélique was a maid of honour to the Queen (an honour also held by Madame de Lafayette); she distorts the facts to exaggerate both the extent of her own early friendship with Angélique, and Angélique's role in attracting the English Queen to Chaillot;[9] and she also refers to the close ties between her uncle, François Motier de Lafayette, and the Queen. Thus from the outset

continuing writing after Madame's death, she should have burned the manuscript (*De l'influence des femmes sur la littérature* (Paris, 1811), 131, cit. Laugaa, 165).

[5] The reference to 'la duchesse de Savoie, aujourd'hui régnante' (21) indicates that the preface was written at some point after Mlle de Valois's marriage to the Duc de Savoie in April 1684.

[6] A. Beaunier suggests that the *Histoire* may have been started as a report for the King, who was conducting an inquiry about Vardes and the Spanish letter (see A. Beaunier, 'Madame de Lafayette et Madame', *Revue de Paris* 33 (1926), 73–100). The sharply critical comments about the King's behaviour, however, make it unlikely that the version that survives was ever intended to be seen by him.

[7] She writes (in the third person) that she had pleased Madame 'par son bonheur; car, bien qu'on lui trouvât du mérite, c'était une sorte de mérite si sérieux en apparence, qu'il ne semblait pas qu'il dût plaire à une princesse aussi jeune que Madame. Cependant, elle lui avait été agréable et elle avait été si touchée du mérite et de l'esprit de Madame, qu'elle lui dût plaire dans la suite par l'attachement qu'elle eut pour elle' (38–9).

[8] 'L'on croyait avoir atteint la perfection, quand on avait su plaire à Madame', said Bossuet in his funeral oration for Henriette (Bossuet, 'Oraison funèbre de Henriette-Anne d'Angleterre, duchesse d'Orléans', in *Oraisons funèbres, panégyriques*, ed. Abbé Velat and Yvonne Champailler (Paris: Gallimard Pléïade, 1961), 87).

[9] See Duchêne, *Madame de Lafayette*, 76–8.

she firmly establishes that the name of Lafayette has long been associated with royal confidences. Of Angélique de Lafayette, she writes: 'Le Roi conserva pour elle beaucoup d'amitié et lui donna sa confiance: ainsi [. . .] elle était très-considérée, et elle le méritait' (20). The text will show that Madame de Lafayette herself enjoys a similar degree of trust and friendship with Madame: the implicit suggestion is that she, like her sister-in-law, deserves to be 'très-considérée'. Since the central concern of the main body of the *Histoire* is the rivalry between courtiers to win confidences from members of the royal family, by acknowledging her authorship Madame de Lafayette announces her own closeness to Madame and displays her status as superior to that of the courtiers about whom she is writing.

As she proclaims her social success while at the same time disclaiming all responsibility for the text, the ambivalence between reticence and self-revelation is mirrored in the text's fluctuating narrative voice. In the preface Madame de Lafayette introduces herself as the sister-in-law of Angélique de Lafayette, and uses the first person freely. Not until the final death-scene (where she plays an important supportive role to Madame, Monsieur and the King) is she again willing consistently to use the 'je' to give an avowedly first-hand account. Most of the main body of the text, including the brief description of herself (38–9), is related in the third person, with occasional first- and second-person interpolations. But the narrative voice of the main sections of the account is a double one: Madame de Lafayette has made it clear that the events described were told first by Madame, and then by herself. Only the 'je' of the preface and the death-scene can therefore be read as Madame de Lafayette's direct expression; the 'je' of the main narrative merges into the 'nous' or hides behind the anonymous third person who can describe Madame de Lafayette and Mademoiselle de la Trimouille in the same breath.

But these hesitations go even further. The doubly female voice of the narrative sometimes switches to a male persona which appeals explicitly to male assumptions. Reading, for example, the comment that 'l'attachement d'une femme est rarement un obstacle à l'amour qu'on a pour une maîtresse' (31), we find ourselves thrust into a male domain where such attitudes are, by implication, commonplace. Elsewhere, however, the 'on' retains a distinctly female voice, as in the reference to 'la jalousie qu'on a d'ordinaire de celles qui ont été aimées de ceux qui nous aiment' (48). In short, Madame de Lafayette's conflicting drives towards self-revelation and self-effacement are not only to be found in her contradictory claims in the preface, but are also embedded in the text itself.

Part One of the *Histoire de Madame* opens, like much of Madame de Lafayette's fiction, with a reference to the relationship between love and war. In this case the account begins with a peace treaty and a marriage treaty: 'La paix était faite entre la France et l'Espagne; le mariage du Roi était achevé après beaucoup de difficultés' (22). One is part and parcel of the other. The *Histoire* resembles most of her fiction in another respect: it opens on a note of closure. The novels and short stories (with the exception of *Zaïde*) begin where most conventional novels end—with a marriage—and the *Histoire*, too, begins with problems apparently resolved. The war is at an end, the King's marriage has at last taken place after difficult negotiations, and Mazarin's career is at the height of its glory. Critics have repeatedly stressed Madame de Lafayette's recurrent preoccupation with the theme of *repos*, a state of calm and tranquillity, and this opening characteristically suggests an awareness of the fragility of such a state. Peace, marriage and success are all seen as precarious, and the poised moment of *repos* with which the work opens is in sharp contrast with the turmoil of passions and politics that will follow. What interests Madame de Lafayette are the undercurrents of conflict that always recur, rather than the exceptional and transitory moment of peace. She will show how inextricably bound up with one another these public and private conflicts are.

In describing the events that follow, Madame de Lafayette goes further in arranging the facts of Madame's account into a form that is closer to fiction. Madame is said to view her flirtation with Guiches as 'de la plaisanterie de roman' (50), and is portrayed as setting her behaviour in a literary context when she tells Vardes that she treats the King as if he were Chabanes (the unrequited suitor in *La Princesse de Montpensier*).[10] Events take a truly romanesque turn when Guiches secretly enters Madame's apartments disguised as a woman fortune-teller and is able to tell the fortunes of the ladies-in-waiting without being recognized (51), and later when he is saved from certain death in battle by a portrait of Madame which deflects the blow (67). The account of Madame's sudden death, too, finds Madame de Lafayette using the techniques of fiction. Unexpected though it was, Madame's

---

[10] The original published version reads: 'Madame lui répondit en plaisantant que, pour le Roi, elle lui permettait le personnage de Chabanes' (71).

death is carefully prepared for in the narrative, and the portrait of her character undergoes a remarkable transformation as the end approaches. From being a charming but mischievous intriguer who is quite prepared to make and break promises and tell lies to get herself out of trouble, she comes to be presented as a model of rectitude, convinced of the value of truth. The ending thus propounds an uplifting moral to the reader (although its ambiguity is not lost on us). All these details, then, show Madame de Lafayette working to make sense of the events, taking imaginative control of them and shaping them to form a pattern with recurrent themes and an underlying message.

One of the most noticeable traits of her narrative is the consistent way in which she seeks to undermine expectations. Although a quest for surprise and discovery is characteristic of *précieux* writing, the *Histoire* does more than just strive for an arresting effect: Madame de Lafayette seems constantly to appeal to received wisdom only to challenge it and propose an alternative perspective. One set of these implied assumptions relates to physical appearance. The expectation presented is that beauty is women's most desirable quality; instead, Madame de Lafayette repeatedly gives instances of women who are desirable although not beautiful, or beautiful yet unappealing. Thus Louis XIV's young Spanish wife is described as someone 'qu'on pouvait appeler belle, quoiqu'elle ne fût pas agréable'(25), like Mademoiselle de Tonnay-Charente who is 'encore une beauté très-achevée, quoiqu'elle ne fût pas parfaitement agréable' (32). The Comtesse de Soissons, on the other hand, is 'une personne qu'on ne pouvait pas appeler belle et qui néanmoins était capable de plaire' (27), just as Madame de Chalais is 'très-aimable sans être fort belle' (37). An even more striking case is Mademoiselle de Mancini, who is not at all beautiful, and of whom we are told that 'il n'y avait nul charme dans sa personne, et très peu dans son esprit', which is 'hardi, résolu, emporté, libertin et éloigné de toute sorte de civilité et de politesse'. Nevertheless, like similar characters in Madame de Lafayette's fiction, she is able to inspire great passion: 'l'on peut dire qu'elle contraignit le Roi à l'aimer' (29). In composing her account, then, Madame de Lafayette will insist far more on the psychological traits of the protagonists than on their appearance: appearances are deceptive, beauty is only skin deep, and the true key to people's character is how they behave rather than how they look. The various disguises they adopt—the Comte de Guiches's exploits dressed as a female fortune-teller or, later, as one of Louise de la Vallière's servants, Puy-Guilhem's pursuit of Madame de Valentinois disguised as a merchant or a postilion, and the masked ball at which the guests fail to recognize one another—all serve to underline the idea that superficial appearances belie the hidden truth.

This emphasis on disguised identity, which recurs, of course, in Madame de Lafayette's fiction, is perhaps not surprising. We know from the memoirs of the Abbé de Choisy, the son of one of her old friends, that Madame de Lafayette encouraged him to dress as a woman and complimented him on his appearance when he did so. 'Mme de Lafayette se crut engagée à faire approuver dans le monde ce qu'elle m'avait conseillé, peut-être un peu légèrement, et je continuai pendant deux mois à m'habiller tous les jours en femme,' he recalls.[11] Her support of the Abbé's gender impersonation, and her fascination with the idea of disguise and with the wider possibilities of behaviour it opens up, are surely functions of her awareness of the freedom which her own, more subtle, authorial 'cross-dressing' gives her.

In the *Histoire de Madame* she repeatedly undermines expectations about how people will behave. Assumptions based on how they have acted in the past are shown to be unreliable bases for predicting how they will react in the future. Thus the Queen-mother, who during her husband's lifetime had appeared to take an anxious interest in affairs of state, is revealed as indolent and lethargic, with 'une assez grande indifférence pour toutes choses' (25) once she is left to her own devices. The King's Spanish bride also turns out to be quite different from what everyone expected, with 'un esprit fort éloigné de ces desseins ambitieux dont on avait tant parlé' (29). Louis XIV himself is equally unpredictable: he is expected to continue to play the passive role he had followed under Mazarin, and when he not only assumes his full powers as monarch but also takes over the functions of prime minister, Madame de Lafayette stresses the general amazement that anyone could change so completely. Her desire to present him in a way other than might be expected leads her to introduce him almost at the end of her list of court portraits, saying that although she ought perhaps to have described him at the outset, 'on ne saurait le

---

[11] See Abbé de Choisy, *Mémoires de l'Abbé de Choisy habillé en femme*, in *Mémoires pour servir à l'Histoire de Louis XIV*, ed. G. Montgrédien (Paris: Mercure de France, 1966); and Duchêne, *Madame de Lafayette*, 268.

dépeindre que par ses actions; et celles que nous avons vues jusqu'au temps dont nous venons de parler étaient si éloignées de celles que nous avons vues depuis, qu'elles ne pourraient guère servir à le faire connaître' (26). Again, predictions based on hasty assumptions are proved wrong.

The same pattern recurs as she relates the protagonists' life-events: they are shown to be as incapable of understanding themselves as of foreseeing what is about to happen to them. The tone is set in the preface with the story of Angélique de la Fayette. A victim of Richelieu's intriguing, she is the King's favourite one moment but has to flee to a convent the next. This pattern persists throughout the work. At the very moment when all Mazarin's stars seem to be in the ascendant, he dies; Mademoiselle de Mancini finds herself being hurriedly packed off to Italy instead of becoming Queen of France; Fouquet is arrested at the height of his triumph. And, of course, Madame has just returned from her important and successful visit to England, happier, more radiant and more admired than ever before, when death intervenes, 'moins attendue qu'un coup de tonnerre' (80).

By preceding Madame's death by all these instances of sudden downfall following a moment of glory, Madame de Lafayette prepares us for the final tragedy. The reader already knows that it will happen, of course—if not through familiarity with this period of French history, then simply because the death is announced in the preface. But the insistent patterning of life-events to form a parallel with Madame's fate is evidence of a manipulation of events to suggest that, unexpected though they may seem, these events are nevertheless driven by a guiding force which the author alone can perceive. Seen from this perspective, ambition and intrigue and petty squabbles seem futile; the magnitude of the final tragedy serves to deflate the jostling for power that goes on in the main body of the text. As a technique, it is to be compared with Madame de Lafayette's use of interpolated stories in her fiction, where the circumstances of lesser characters act as parallels, contrasts or warnings for the main protagonists.

This emphasis on the unexpected and the inexplicable in the lives of individuals is symptomatic of Madame de Lafayette's vision of historical events, where the individual fortunes of the protagonists correspond to a pattern which also shapes the wider world. Fortune is as fickle as the inconstant lovers who crowd the book. A prime instance is the revolution in England—'un exemple de l'inconstance de la fortune qui est su de toute la terre' (34)—which almost as suddenly and inexplicably reverses itself to restore Charles II to the throne (35). The same pattern runs through the later *Mémoires de la cour de France*, where major events of national and international importance are shown to be unpredicted and unprepared for; it is a pattern which also marks Madame de Lafayette's later fictional narratives, where the characters find themselves constantly surprised by their own emotional reactions. So Madame de Lafayette's account stresses its author's ability to unravel a tangled web of seemingly incomprehensible characters and actions. The interwoven intrigues may seem impenetrable to the uncomprehending public, as she frequently implies, but she, as writer, is in the all-powerful position of being able to tease out the details, correct mistaken assumptions, reveal and explain.

A major guiding theme is located in the acquisition of power in all its guises. Madame de Lafayette relates in passing the changes in the main power-structure of the nation: Mazarin's rise to supremacy during the Queen-mother's regency; Louis XIV's assumption of control after Mazarin's death; the rivalry between his chief ministers, culminating in the plot to oust Fouquet; the fighting in Lorraine and in Poland; and, in the shadowy background, the English revolution and restoration of the monarchy. But it is not this 'public' power that most interests her. Instead, she presents a minutely detailed picture of power-struggles in the private sphere, showing that interwoven with the political events runs a network of intrigue which uses love—or the appearance of love—as a means to power. The casket of Fouquet's papers seized after his arrest is the perfect metaphor for this: it turns out to contain more love letters than official documents. As Madame de Lafayette describes it, the most devastating consequences of his downfall come not so much from the disclosure of his official papers as from the revelation of these clandestine amours (46).

She introduces the idea at an early stage by means of a play on the words *maître* and *maîtresse*. The young King, still under the thumb of Mazarin, whose influence extends to emotional as well as political affairs, falls in love with Mademoiselle de Mancini. He is so devoted to her (the phrase Madame de Lafayette uses, significantly, is 'il *se soumit* si absolument') that she is his mistress in both senses of the word: 'l'on peut dire qu'elle fut la maîtresse d'un prince que nous avons vu depuis maître de sa maîtresse et de son amour' (23).

Establishing at the outset that the King will ultimately assume absolute control, Madame de Lafayette nevertheless persists in presenting him as a weak figure who can easily be dominated, constrained or deceived. Mademoiselle de Mancini *forces* him to fall in love with her, we are told,[12] and has over him 'le plus absolu pouvoir qu'une maîtresse ait jamais eu sur le cœur d'un amant' (24). Later, she reproaches him for shedding ineffectual tears instead of acting with authority. Madame de Lafayette's *Histoire* makes it clear that the King's power lies in his status rather than in his inherent character. Nevertheless, he is the ultimate focus of the other court members' desire for power. He is the *maître*, but they will try to gain influence over him—or, in the case of the women, attempt to become his *maîtresse*, which will amount to the same thing.[13]

But the King is by no means the only focus for the desire for power. In Madame de Lafayette's portrayal of court life it is the royal women rather than the men who are in the most influential positions. She presents Monsieur as something of a joke, effeminate, ineffectual and easily dominated by those around him. He is 'si susceptible d'impressions, que les personnes qui l'approchaient pouvaient quasi répondre de s'en rendre maîtres, en le prenant par son faible' (26). Madame, on the other hand, begins to recognize 'la *puissance* de ses charmes' (35) shortly before her marriage to Monsieur, and when she then emerges into the public eye she immediately becomes the focus of attention and ambition for the entire court: 'Ce fut alors que toute la France se trouva chez elle; tous les hommes ne pensaient qu'à lui faire leur cour, et toutes les femmes qu'à lui plaire' (38).

The Queen-mother is said by Madame de Lafayette to hold the top position in the royal household, although she chooses not to wield her power: after her husband's death, 'dès qu'elle avait été maîtresse et d'elle même et du royaume', she prefers to live a quiet life, uninvolved in public affairs. Nevertheless she is shown to exert a powerful but hidden influence over the King, who fears her (53). She is one of several women described here whose power stems in part from the fact that they are their own mistresses. The Comtesse de Soissons is another. She was the King's first love; she is 'incapable de s'assujétir qu'à ce qui lui était agréable' and 'si peu capable de se contraindre'

---

[12] '... l'on peut dire qu'elle contraignit le Roi à l'aimer' (29).
[13] Cf. the repeated play on the words *maître* and *maîtresse* with reference to the King, Madame de la Vallière and the Comtesse de Soissons (53–4).

(28) that she has the nerve and daring necessary to pursue her ambitious intrigues. In that description of her we recognize shades of the other successfully independent women, such as Madame de Noirmoutier or Madame de Valentinois, who play such an important role in Madame de Lafayette's fictional world.

Madame de Lafayette is careful to show that the men and the women she describes have similar ambitions although their apparent objectives are different: 'Ainsi beaucoup de gens espéraient quelque part aux affaires; et beaucoup de dames, *par des raisons à peu près semblables*, espéraient beaucoup de part aux bonnes grâces du Roi' (24). The women may not play an explicit part in affairs of state, but they are shown to exert at least as much influence through their operations in the emotional sphere. Thus Madame de Lafayette brackets together 'les ministres qui pouvaient prétendre au gouvernement de l'Etat et les dames qui pouvaient aspirer aux bonnes grâces du Roi' (24). These ladies have as their model the memory of Gabrielle d'Estrées, the mistress for whom Henri IV sought the annulment of his marriage to Marguerite de Valois. In the courtly games and ritualistic manœuvres that characterize their jockeying for position, sincerity plays little part. The 'passions' and 'love-affairs' are, as often as not, merely strategic devices devoid of real emotional involvement. It is therefore hardly surprising that some of the strongest feelings Madame de Lafayette paints are those which derive from jealousy rather than love. Jealousy implies rivalry, and is inevitable in any struggle for status or power.[14]

But real power, it is clear, works through language. The most adept manipulators at court are those who are able to extract confidences and pass on information or misinformation. Madame de Lafayette repeatedly shows people gaining a position of control by generating and proliferating information through either the spoken or the written word. In some cases they can aspire to the highest level by these means. The unscrupulous Montalais is the prime example. She knows how to play with language, and is able to lead a conversation with the Comte de Guiches through so many twists and turns that he confesses

---

[14] Note that the King is shown to be unable to bear rivalry. As soon as he suspects that a mistress is interested in another man he discards her. See the incidents concerning Mademoiselle de Mancini and the nephew of the Duc de Lorraine (31), and the Comtesse de Soissons and M. de Villequier (28). Louis refuses to engage in a power struggle: his position must remain above question.

that he loves Madame (49). Montalais's next step is to exploit this little piece of information by inflating its importance and disseminating it: she wants to 'donner un air d'importance à cette galanterie' and thinks that if she can spread her information widely enough, she will be in a supremely influential position: 'elle composerait une intrigue qui gouvernerait l'Etat' (51). Her talent for eliciting confidences is prodigious: in spite of the King's disapproval, she soon has Madame, Louise de la Vallière and Mademoiselle de Tonnay-Charente all confiding their secrets to her: 'Une seule de ces confidences eût pu occuper une personne entière, et Montalais seule suffisait à toutes' (50). Moreover, she even manages to persuade the suspicious King to confide in her as well (53).

If confidences, true and false, are circulated, private feelings are entrusted to letters, which themselves then become elements in the quest for power. They accumulate, and have to be retrieved through more intriguing, for to be in control of a compromising letter is to be in a position of power. When suitably compromising letters do not exist, they sometimes have to be invented, and so forgery and blackmail enter the list of tactics. As the *Histoire de Madame* unfolds, so the secret information and intrigues multiply. Private comments are repeated and misrepeated, letters are invented, rumours are initiated. By the end of the third part of the account, the language of intrigue has become so dense as to be almost impenetrable.

But then, suddenly, at the beginning of Part Four, a new procedure appears. Instead of pursuing these intrigues, Madame starts to extricate herself. She begins to tell the truth, regardless of its consequences, knowing that only the whole truth can justify her past behaviour: 'Madame se tira de ce labyrinthe en disant toujours la vérité, et sa sincérité la maintint auprès du Roi' (75). Discourse ceases to proliferate: by telling the truth, Madame cuts through the web of intrigue, and by refusing to accept letters, she stems the written flow. The correspondence starts up again briefly after her chance meeting with the Comte de Guiches at the masked ball, but soon the deflationary process is in operation again. She tells the King all she knows, and insists that the Comte de Guiches make a sincere confession of everything, 'ayant trouvé que, dans toutes les matières embrouillées, la vérité seule tire les gens d'affaire' (78). He in turn asks Montalais for the truth, but here the account begins to fade: 'vous saurez ce détail d'elle', we read, but Madame's death intervenes and Montalais never reappears. It is particularly significant that the speaking of the truth, the confession to someone in authority, should here be presented as a means to power; it is a procedure similar to that which will be found in the other confession scenes which punctuate Madame de Lafayette's fiction.

The process that she is describing, then, is a multi-layered one. A nugget of fact is taken by one of the protagonists and turned into a secretive discourse which circulates and expands to gigantic proportions. As it does so, it confers increasing power on the protagonist for as long as he or she (and it is more often a woman) is able to control it. Madame, although the object of many of these intrigues, nevertheless finally rises above them, first by denying them their secretive status by confessing the truth, and second, by recounting them to Madame de Lafayette in (we must assume) her own version. But Madame dies, relinquishing her control of events. Significantly, her death is described as a relinquishing of *speech*: 'elle [. . .] perdit la parole et la vie quasi en même temps; [. . .] après deux ou trois petits mouvements convulsifs dans la bouche, elle expira' (107). Language falters and dies, with the text.

The third, and most important, level on which power is appropriated is through the narrative of the *Histoire de Madame* itself. It is ultimately Madame de Lafayette herself who assumes the role of proliferator of discourse. By shaping the account, passing judgement, displaying and no doubt suppressing details, she is controlling our understanding of events. A process inherent in the writing of *any* history is here made quite explicit. Throughout the text she shows members of the court using the transforming power of narrative as a means of furthering their own ambitions: they take charge of the flux of events by shaping them into written or spoken versions—into accurate or mendacious confidences or letters—and then spread these accounts to serve their own ends. The practice, however, is also shown to be a hazardous one. Generating rumours and writing letters may be ways of exercising authority, but they can also expose their authors to danger. If discovered, the authors risk punishment or disgrace: the versions of events they have created for their own ends can be turned against them. We see repeated instances of letters falling into the wrong hands and so bringing public shame to their author, or of the instigator of a rumour being found out and punished. Thus the *Histoire* becomes a metaphor for the power and risk inherent in the act of writing. In other words, the act of creation creates hostages to fortune.

In the portrait of Madame de Sévigné we saw Madame de Lafayette making the teasing proposition that a named author is subject to risk, and confidently exploiting the benefits of anonymity while signing her name to the piece. Her subsequent work displays a more genuine ambivalence. The tensions and ambiguities present in her fiction suggest conflicting values at which she can only hint. In the *Histoire*, however, her hesitation between self-effacement and self-exposure, between denying and proclaiming her authorship, is even more evident. That hesitation, discernible in the preface, is dramatized in the main body of the text through her focus on both the positive and negative consequences of writing: she shows it to be at once a means to power and a potential danger. Torn between their desire for active engagement and their fear of disgrace, the men and women at the court of Louis XIV, like the heroines of her fiction, are projections of the dilemma facing Madame de Lafayette herself, as woman and author.

At the end of her life Madame de Lafayette again turned to the writing of history. In 1731, thirty-eight years after her death, her *Mémoires de la cour de France pour les années 1688 et 1689* appeared in print. They were accompanied by a publisher's preface claiming that the manuscript, found among Madame de Lafayette's son's papers, was only a fragment of a much larger work in which she had described 'tout ce qui s'était passé à la Cour de France, depuis sa première jeunesse'. The publisher expressed the hope that those in possession of the missing sections of manuscript would soon produce them. But no more of the *Mémoires* ever appeared, and nothing is known for sure of the circumstances in which they were written. It is clear, however, that they were a very different undertaking from the *Histoire de Madame*. The *Histoire* was begun when Madame de Lafayette was near the beginning of her literary career, whereas the *Mémoires* were written within four years of her death. In the *Histoire* she describes events in which she was often directly involved, writes about people she knows and comments on motives and morals. During the period when the *Mémoires* must have been written, however, she was largely confined to her room by illness, and was kept informed about what was happening in the world through letters and visits.[15] In the *Mémoires*,

---

[15] Her informants may well have included her friend Louvois, one of Louis XIV's chief advisers, whose name appears frequently in the *Mémoires*. See Jean Lemoine,

therefore, much of the narrative is given over to accounts of battles, political manœuvres and international intrigues about which she could have known only at second or third hand. The first impression the *Mémoires* give is of a much more conventional piece of writing than the *Histoire de Madame*. But as we read, the focus gradually changes and Madame de Lafayette's familiar detached irony becomes more apparent.

The *Mémoires* begin with an evocation of a France at peace: 'La France était dans une tranquillité parfaite; l'on n'y connaissait plus d'autres armes que les instruments nécessaires pour remuer les terres et pour bâtir' (105). This opening reference to peace and war is so typical of how Madame de Lafayette starts her writings that it seems unlikely that the memoirs are in fact a fragment of a larger work, as the publisher had suggested. Instead, the beginning appears to be a deliberate introduction which sets a less than celebratory perspective for the rest of the account: the description of French troops working on the grandiose project of constructing perpetual fountains for the palace of Versailles establishes a firm basis against which subsequent events will be measured. That over-ambitious scheme involves diverting the river Eure to make it flow 'contre son gré', a project as unnatural as confidence in a lengthy peace. Convinced that there is no risk of war unless France herself declares it, no one gives a thought to the fact that the troops working on the fountains are being debilitated by diseases supposedly originating in the excavated soil and are in no state to be used in a military emergency. Madame de Lafayette's perspective, however, is one of superior knowledge: her reference to 'le sein de la tranquillité dont on jouissait' conveys the characteristic sense of a *repos* which she knows to be precarious and illusory. Her vivid description of the immense expense, effort and suffering involved in offering the King 'le plaisir tout pur de jouir de ses travaux' stands as an emblem of the contrast between immediate personal gratification and long-term suffering which will run through the text.[16]

'Madame de La Fayette et Louvois', *Revue de Paris*, 14ᵉ année, no. 17 (1 Sept. 1907), 65–86. Cf. also Madame de Sévigné's letter of 2 Mar. 1689 describing a visit to Madame de Lafayette's house, where she meets a group of present or former diplomats. 'On y a fort politiqué', she writes.

[16] Later she describes how the two battalions of troops working on the Versailles project are too ill to be sent to defend Cherbourg (124).

By opening the *Mémoires* with a description of the construction work at Versailles,[17] Madame de Lafayette firmly roots her account at the court. Although she will tell of events that range far and wide, over the French countryside and abroad, everything is related from the confined perspective of a narrator who remains at or near the court. Consequently the *Mémoires* set up an intriguing contrast between the domestic and wider spheres. Initially they concentrate on major political issues—the war of the League of Augsburg, the selection of the Elector of Cologne, disputes with the Pope, the worsening European situation, threats to the British monarchy—but these are not eye-witness accounts. On the other hand, Madame de Lafayette also describes the situation of those—particularly the women—who are left behind and wait for news of the action. So although the narrative focuses mainly on military campaigns and political negotiations beyond the immediate scope of the author's experience, her marginal presence is implicitly conveyed by details (which become increasingly common as the *Mémoires* progress) showing the effect of these events on the women left behind, who can only speculate about what may be happening in the wider world. Madame de Lafayette gives as much weight to the private, domestic consequences of international affairs as she does to their political implications.

She shows how the war affects the wives left at home. She describes how the Prince de Conti's young bride has not smiled and has barely spoken since her husband left for battle (130), and how Madame d'Antin collapses in church as news of the victory at Philisbourg is passed to the King by an advance courier: knowing that the news should have been brought by her husband, she assumes (wrongly) that he has been killed or injured (122). The anecdote about Madame la Duchesse, daughter of the King and Madame de Montespan, offers a particularly clear picture of the constraints under which the women live. Madame la Duchesse's father-in-law has her watched, and is told that a man has been seen surreptitiously leaving her home. It

---

[17] In 1671 the King had taken Madame de Lafayette on a personal tour of an earlier stage of the Versailles construction work. 'Elle y fut reçue très bien, mais très bien,' notes Madame de Sévigné, 'c'est à dire que le roi la fit mettre sans sa calèche avec les dames, et prit plaisir à lui montrer toutes les beautés de Versailles comme un particulier que l'on va voir dans sa maison de campagne. Il ne parla qu'à elle, et reçut avec beaucoup de plaisir et de politesse toutes les louanges qu'elle donna aux merveilleuses beautés qu'il lui montrait' (cit. Duchêne, *Madame de Lafayette*, 292).

transpires that Madame la Duchesse had spent the day with Madame de Valentinois, who had secretly sent for a painter to paint her portrait in miniature. In the end the King is asked to intervene to make Madame la Duchesse behave with more propriety; he dismisses her favourite ladies-in-waiting, orders that she should spend all her time in the presence of her mother-in-law, and forbids her to have any visitors in her apartments at Chantilly. Although Madame de Lafayette ends this series of sanctions with the comment: 'Rien de tout cela ne fut exécuté, hormis qu'elle n'eût plus la compagnie de ses filles' (179), her description of the physical confinement of these women, spied on, supervised, scolded and controlled, stands in marked contrast to the geographical range of the armies and consequently of the narrative itself. Madame de Lafayette's history, then, is written through a double optic: the wide overview of official history that chronicles national events, and the more intimate close-up glimpses of domestic life.

That double perspective is reflected in the language of the narrative itself. On the one hand the author appears to identify with the French army and the French cause, frequently using the first-person-plural form to explain the state of affairs: 'nous étions rassurés par l'état de la République de Hollande [. . .] Nous étions donc persuadés que, si la guerre commençait, ce ne pourrait être que par nous' (106). On the other hand she also maintains a detached and critical stance, describing the course of distant events from the often censorious viewpoint of those left behind to speculate and comment on them.

This latter perspective eventually dominates. From her detached position, Madame de Lafayette presents the political and military exploits as a morass of confusion and disorder. Incompetence is as endemic in the power structure as the diseases which were believed to have spread from the exposed soil of the Versailles excavations. Time and again she reports failures like that of M. de Chanlay, who is sent to negotiate with the Pope but who 'eut le malheur de ne pas réussir'. He is passed back and forth between the two men with whom he is supposed to be dealing, and eventually has to return to France without accomplishing anything—as Madame de Lafayette puts it, 'sans avoir vu que l'Italie' (112). When she describes the outbreak of hostilities, she concentrates on bungled details such as the death of the son of M. de Courtin, killed by his own side because he does not know the rallying cry (118); or the injury that the Maréchal de Camp, Harcourt, receives when he slips and falls from the fortifications (120); or the incident where a bored officer of the King's regiment fires at some snipe but accidentally hits and kills the young Chevalier de Longueville (122). Those in command are seen as lacking in judgement: coastal defences have been neglected because the Anglo-Dutch coalition had not been anticipated; of M. de Louvois she writes: 'les vues fort éloignées ne sont pas de son goût' (135); military finances are in complete disarray (154); military leaders meeting at Frankfurt hold many councils of war but make no decisions as each is arguing out of self-interest (180); and command of the navy is taken from the able and experienced Maréchal d'Estrées and given instead to M. de Seignelay, who spends his time gambling and womanizing (182–3). The *Mémoires* end with a naval disaster and a wry comment: 'Voilà à quoi se termina pour lors l'exploit de la plus formidable armée que le Roi eût jusqu'à présent mise sur mer' (190).

Those in ultimate authority do not escape this critical presentation. Although Madame de Lafayette does not make the point explicitly, her account of the blunders and confusion of the day-to-day running of the war paints a picture of the incompetence of the great. The Pope is roundly criticized: 'il s'est bien écarté de cette voie d'équité et de justice, que doit avoir un bon père pour ses enfants', and his behaviour over the appointment of the Elector of Cologne is 'pas pardonnable, ni même excusable' (108). James II of England is presented as negligent, paying no heed to warnings and spending time at the hunt or pursuing his religious fanaticism instead of attending to more important affairs: 'Plus les Français voyaient le roi d'Angleterre, moins on le plaignait de la perte de son royaume: ce prince n'était obsédé que des jésuites' (149). Louis XIV, too, has been neglectful, over-preoccupied with erecting buildings and fountains when everything around him seems set to crumble (134).

From time to time Madame de Lafayette is obliged to record certain successes, but she shows them to be exceptional, brought about by good fortune rather than good management. Whereas in the *Histoire de Madame* chance seemed regularly to intervene to cut short an individual's success (as in the cases of Mazarin, Mademoiselle de Mancini, Fouquet, Madame, etc.), here the reverse is the case: only by sheer luck are disasters averted. The description of Louis XIV's passion for the fashionable new game of 'portiques', a pastime which, comments Madame de Lafayette, requires no more skill than playing heads-or-tails, is emblematic of the many instances where chance, and not intellect, rules. A fortuitous nosebleed prevents James II from attending a dinner at which he was to have been handed over to William of Orange (132); the ship carrying the Queen of England to safety in France blunders into the middle of the Dutch fleet, but is not recognized in the darkness (138); the King of England, crossing the channel in a small vessel, fears that a larger ship bearing down on him will attack, but it turns out to be a French boat coming to rescue him; although Seignelay mismanages the navy at Brest, the expected defeats are averted by 'un coup du ciel' (185). Confusion and mismanagement are the order of the day, success is accidental, and the admiring superlatives which peppered the *Histoire de Madame* are here virtually absent.

As the *Mémoires* progress, the tone becomes increasingly jaundiced. Madame de Lafayette paints a picture of universal disintegration. The peace that had once been thought stable is swiftly eroded, the whole of Europe is in turmoil, France is threatened on all sides, and disorder reigns on the battlefields. Only at court does the old order remain. But Madame de Lafayette has little sympathy with a stultifying order where life goes on unchanged and with the same boring predictability: 'A l'égard de la cour de France, tout y était comme à l'ordinaire. Il y a un certain train qui ne changeait point: toujours les mêmes plaisirs, toujours aux mêmes heures, et toujours avec les mêmes gens' (141). Her account moves back and forth between the sheltered court and the troubled areas around France's borders, suggesting that disorder will inevitably spread to the court itself despite those who cling blindly to the old rituals.

Disputes about precedence are common, and Madame de Lafayette notes that the arguments about the prerogatives of women's rank are more difficult to resolve than those of men (147). If she describes them at considerable length, it is because these disputes over privileges such as the shape of one's chair represent competition for precedence and rank, hence power and prestige: refusals to acknowledge new social positions reflect resistance to inevitable changes in the old order. Arguments about precedence are the domestic counterpart of the power struggles between nations and are treated as a reflection of those warlike times. Madame de Lafayette does not fail to note that in the presentation of the seventy-three new Cordons-Bleus 'les gens de guerre y eurent beaucoup de part, parce qu'on voyait bien que l'on allait avoir besoin d'eux', or that the allocation of the honours has been decided by M. de Louvois, one of the King's chief advisers on the war (132). Time and again she intermingles peace with war, always ready to intersperse accounts of battles with private conflicts, and to present life at court as a microcosm of the wider troubles. For example, her long account of the deployment of commanders and troops and the declaration of war on the Prince of Orange is interrupted by the story of the turbulent relationship between the Comte de Brionne and his mistress which ends in a duel between Brionne and the lady's brother. And the 'grande affaire' of M. de Marsan's attempt to take revenge on Madame la Duchesse by pretending to be an ardent admirer, and the account of further minor power struggles involving the same lady, immediately precede a detailed report of military campaigns. Despite the 'tranquillité parfaite' evoked in the opening sentence of the *Mémoires*, in both public and private life conflict is now shown to be the order of the day.

In one of the most remarkable passages of the book Madame de Lafayette describes Madame de Maintenon's school for young girls at St-Cyr. It is an establishment worthy of both the King and its founder, she writes, adding acidly, 'mais quelquefois les choses les mieux instituées dégénèrent considérablement' (150). The disintegration she foresees at St-Cyr reflects her wider view of French society. This seat of virtue and piety will soon become a place of debauchery because its 300 girls are living in such close proximity to a court 'remplie de gens éveillés': it is unreasonable to expect young men and women to live so close together without scaling the walls to get to each other, she writes.

The inflexible order which Madame de Maintenon attempts to instil at St-Cyr seems to exemplify the rigidity of life at court, where even 'les plaisirs' have lost their sparkle.[18] Madame de Lafayette drains the word of its true meaning as she describes the performance at the newly built Trianon of an opera whose 'vers [. . .] étaient trèsmauvais, et la musique des plus médiocres'; Louis invites the King and Queen of England to watch it, 'et leur donna *ce plaisir*'(149–50). The King spends his time hunting, playing billiards or engrossed in the undemanding game of 'portiques'. Court balls are so dull that they never last for more than two hours, and religiosity is gaining ground.

---

[18] After a period of mourning for the death of the Queen of Spain, 'l'on croyait que les appartements recommenceraient [. . .]; mais le Roi retrancha ces plaisirs, et dit qu'il avait beaucoup d'affaires; que l'heure des appartements était celle qui lui convenait le plus pour travailler [. . .]: ainsi ce fut là une occupation de moins pour les courtisans' (160).

Madame de Lafayette depicts the court as austere and oppressive, dangerously withdrawing into itself, ever repeating the same rituals. Moreover, she recognizes that there is a relationship between stultifying social circumstances and a loss of creativity. Even Racine, 'le meilleur poète du temps', is obliged to turn from writing incomparable plays to writing history; as a playwright he is described as 'inimitable', but as a historian he is 'très-imitable'—no longer unique or exceptional, but indistinguishable from many others. Commissioned by Madame de Maintenon to write a comedy on a pious subject for the pupils at St-Cyr, he produces *Esther*, which Madame de Lafayette considers to be all very well for little girls, but certainly not worthy of the extravagant praise heaped upon it to flatter Madame de Maintenon: 'Ce qui devait être regardé comme une comédie de couvent devint l'affaire la plus sérieuse de la Cour'(151). Because it is seen as an allegory of the rise of Madame de Maintenon and the eclipse of the King's previous mistress, Madame de Montespan, the play enjoys an enormous success: ministers leave aside the most pressing affairs of state to attend, and 'il n'y eut ni petit ni grand qui n'y voulût aller' (151). Madame de Lafayette shows clearly that the disproportionate acclaim it attracts is simply a manifestation of the rush to curry favour with the new royal mistress. To heap extravagant praise on *Esther* is a way of ensuring a position of favour in the court's austere new social framework.

As Madame de Lafayette makes clear, Racine's unrivalled literary skills have been reduced to the service of court politics. The great period of artistic patronage, mistresses and displays of magnificence is over,[19] and the court is seen as inhibiting creative invention. No longer is it peopled with men and women who can be described as exceptional or outstanding or superlative. Unlike the *Histoire de Madame*, whose characters teem with imaginative intrigues and literary invention, the *Mémoires de la cour de France* paint a picture of a society where little room is left for originality or creativity. Like Racine, Madame de Lafayette had turned from her 'inimitable' fiction to the writing of a historical chronicle. It was to be the last work she wrote.

---

[19] See Robin Briggs, *Early Modern France 1560–1715* (Oxford: Oxford University Press, 1977), 159.

CHAPTER 3

❖

La Comtesse de Tende

Like the manuscript of the *Mémoires de la cour de France*, the austere tale of the Comtesse de Tende was found among Louis de Lafayette's papers after his death. It was first published in 1724 but may well have been written between 1658 and 1660.[1] Set almost a century earlier, *La Comtesse de Tende* is a short story which on a first reading seems to be a very simple little tale of rapidly unfolding events. The Comte de Tende neglects his young bride and is soon unfaithful to her. Initially jealous and passionate, she soon ceases to care. The Count's friend, the Chevalier de Navarre, asks the Countess to act as an intermediary in his courtship of her close friend, the Princesse de Neufchâtel. The Countess agrees, but soon she and Navarre fall in love with each other. Their affair continues in secret after Navarre's marriage to the Princesse de Neufchâtel, but when Navarre is killed in battle, leaving the Countess pregnant, she confesses to her husband, gives birth to a baby who does not survive, and dies.

The tale has been strangely neglected by critics. All too often it is discussed only in relation to *La Princesse de Clèves*—as an inferior and abbreviated attempt to explore the same questions of passion versus duty, marital infidelity, and the problem of confession. *La Comtesse de Tende* is generally seen as a trial run, interesting only as a prototype for the masterpiece. Yet when it was first published, it was paid rather more attention. Commentators fastened on to the moral lesson being preached, and were pleased to find this more clearly defined than in *La Princesse de Clèves*. *La Comtesse de Tende*, they argued, showed the unambiguous downfall of an adulteress whose suffering, guilt and death constituted a clear warning to any reader who might be contemplating similar behaviour. The anonymous author of an introduction to the short story in the *Bibliothèque universelle des romans* in 1776 went so far as to suggest that *La Comtesse de Tende* was the most

---

[1] See Alain Niderst, 'Introduction' to Madame de Lafayette, *Romans et nouvelles*, ed. E. Magne (Paris: Garnier, 1970), p. xliii.

worthy monument to the memory of Madame de Lafayette, 'puisqu'il fut composé dans des intentions aussi honorables'.[2] It remained popular during the first part of the nineteenth century when it was seen as both moral and touching, but in the latter half of the century critics rarely mentioned it, preferring to overlook what they considered to be Madame de Lafayette's lapse of decorum in writing too explicitly about sexual matters. More recently, the few critics who devote more than a passing reference to *La Comtesse de Tende* continue to see it essentially as a moral treatise whose portrayal of the suffering of an adulterous woman offers an unambiguous warning to the reader. Micheline Cuénin, in an article entitled 'La terreur sans la pitié: *La Comtesse de Tende*', argues that the story is a moral condemnation of the Countess, whose loss of self-control is contrasted with the wisdom, reason and restraint of her husband. Cuénin maintains that the Countess is presented as wholly responsible for her own downfall, and because of this didactic moral perspective, she sees Madame de Lafayette as a 'médecin de l'âme'.[3] All these interpretations view the tale as straightforward, moral and unproblematic and, in the process, stress the author's criticism of women as feeble, fickle and lustful, weakly or wantonly breaking moral codes and receiving just punishment.

But *La Comtesse de Tende* is far from being so unambiguous a cautionary tale. It has been argued that the plot is the almost literal account of the life of the Duchesse de Roquelaure, who died in childbirth in 1658 after having betrayed her husband with Monsieur de Vardes.[4] If this is so, we must ask ourselves why the story has been transferred into the past, and, in particular, into that specific historical past. Of course questions of delicacy and propriety arise: discretion would require the protagonists' identities to be disguised, and what better way to do this than to have the events happen before the real-life characters were born? But given that, why was the first year of the reign of Catherine de Médicis chosen as the starting-point for the story, and why was the Duchesse de Roquelaure given the name of Mademoiselle de Strozzi, who, far from being an adulteress, was,

---

[2] (Paris: Lacombe, Jan. 1776), 186–8, cit. J. W. Scott, 'Criticism and *La Comtesse de Tende*', *Modern Language Review* 50 (Jan. 1955), 15–24 (esp. 18).

[3] Micheline Cuénin, 'La terreur sans la pitié: *La Comtesse de Tende*', *Revue d'histoire littéraire de la France* 77 (1977), 478–99.

[4] Niderst, 'Introduction', pp. xlii–xliii.

according to Brantôme, one of the most 'honnêtes, belles, bonnes, courageuses' of ladies, held in the highest esteem at court, and who drowned in 1564 after falling overboard from Charles IX's galley off the coast of Marseilles?

The answer would seem to lie in the associations conjured up by this historical placement. The regency of Catherine de Médicis was a period when peace was constantly threatened. It was a time when the power and strength of women was in evidence (disturbingly so, in the view of many commentators), not only in France but also in Scotland and England, where Mary Queen of Scots and Elizabeth I were on their thrones.[5] The heroine, then, is implicitly identified with these powerful and disruptive currents by her close relationship to Catherine de Médicis. Moreover, the unquestioned virtue of the real Mademoiselle de Strozzi and her blameless and tragic death lie deep beneath the unfolding fiction, hinting, as we shall see, at an alternative moral judgement to the one perceived with such certainty by eighteenth-century readers.

In the story, Madame de Lafayette explores the interplay between sanctioned and unsanctioned behaviour—between that which is socially approved and that which is not—and shows all four of the main characters seeking ways of reconciling their passions and ambitions with the demands of an implicit external authority. Their dilemmas emphasize the differences between the constraints which court society imposes on men and women, and the differences in their responses to those constraints—a frequent subject for exploration in Madame de Lafayette's writings. While it is acceptable for a man to be unfaithful to his wife, both are dishonoured in the eyes of the public if she is known to be unfaithful to him. It is therefore female behaviour which is potentially more disruptive to the social order, and Madame de Lafayette portrays women who are less concerned or less able to preserve that apparent order than are the men. It is, however, far from evident that she is critical of that fact. The message that emerges from the tale is that maintenance of the social order is incompatible with honesty and depends instead upon secrecy and dissimulation: what the world does not know, it cannot condemn. The moral is hardly an edifying one.

---

[5] See Ian Maclean, *Woman Triumphant. Feminism in French Literature 1610–1652* (Oxford: Clarendon Press, 1977), 58.

Tensions between order and disruption are already present in the long and extraordinary opening sentence: 'Mademoiselle de Strozzi, fille du maréchal et proche parente de Cathérine de Médicis, épousa, la première année de la Régence de cette reine, le comte de Tende, de la maison de Savoie, riche, bien fait, le seigneur de la cour qui vivait avec le plus d'éclat et plus propre à se faire estimer qu'à plaire' (399).[6] At first sight, this opening appears to set the young woman firmly within the approved order of the court: we learn her father's name and status, her royal connections, her wealthy marriage to a handsome man of similar standing. But three details alert us to alternative possibilities. First, her Italian ancestry is strongly suggestive of passion and spontaneity (as Madame de Lafayette emphasizes a few lines later) and so is associated with the overthrow of approved 'womanly virtues'.[7] Second, her close relationship to Catherine de Médicis associates her with that archetype of the strong-willed, independent woman whose influence over French politics lasted for almost thirty years, and whose reign was associated with conflict and disorder. And third, the ironic deflation with which the sentence comes to its close highlights the dual perspective from which the story will be written: the list of qualities which appear to make the Count outstandingly eligible as a husband ends with 'et plus propre à se faire estimer qu'à plaire'—his attributes of wealth, beauty, prestige and display attract public esteem, but he is not a likeable man. The story's title, *La Comtesse de Tende*, therefore carries a double message. On the surface it evokes a cluster of social assumptions about marriage, status, lineage and woman's role, but subsumed within that name are the connotations of power, passion and disorder associated with the names of Strozzi and Médicis. The story will unfold to show the Countess attempting, unsuccessfully, to reconcile the two conflicting orders—anarchical power on the one hand, social con-

[6] Page numbers in brackets refer to the Garnier edition of Madame de Lafayette's *Romans et Nouvelles*—see above, n. 1.

[7] The point is stressed again in the same paragraph: 'La comtesse de Tende, vive, et d'une race italienne, devint jalouse.' In his *De l'éducation des filles* (1687), ed. C. Defodon (Paris: Hachette, 1881), Fénelon expressly forbade the teaching of Spanish and Italian, 'car ces deux langues ne servent guère qu'à lire des livres dangereux et capables d'augmenter les défauts des femmes; [. . .] dans l'italien et dans l'espagnol [. . .] règne un jeu d'esprit et une vivacité d'imagination sans règle' (121–2). Madame de Lafayette, however, learned to read and speak Italian; Ménage wrote love-poems to her in Italian, and she likened herself to Petrarch's Laura. See *Corr.* i. 83 (to Ménage, 12 Dec. 1656).

vention and repute on the other—which 'Strozzi/Médicis' and 'Tende' imply.

If I have dwelt at some length on the first sentence, it is because it provides a good example of the multiple layers of meaning in Madame de Lafayette's work, and an illustration of the tensions and contradictions within the text which suggest that, far from presenting a straightforward condemnation of 'les désordres de l'amour' in favour of order and tranquillity, she is hinting at an alternative and barely articulable perspective on the events narrated. But, as is observed within the story itself, the unarticulated can be 'plus parlant que les paroles' (400).

The only character to break deliberately and overtly with social convention is the Princesse de Neufchâtel. At the start of the story she is in the position of greatest prestige: she is young, rich and beautiful, and from her late husband she has acquired 'cette souveraineté qui la rendait le parti de la cour le plus élevé et le plus brillant' (399). Despite her powerful position she decides to marry beneath her for love, fully aware that she will incur general disapproval. She makes only a token gesture towards trying to avoid 'l'improbation de tout le monde'—by keeping her marriage to Navarre secret until after it has taken place, she merely delays the disapproval and forestalls any attempt to dissuade her. Her subsequent distress comes not from having flouted public opinion, nor from having made 'un mariage inégal, désapprouvé, qui [l]'abaisse' (404), but from her fear that her new husband does not in fact love her, and that her sacrifice may have been in vain. Interestingly, however, the last mention of the Princess presents her as 'contente de son mari' and inspiring jealousy in the Countess (407).

The Comte de Tende's behaviour is at the opposite extreme to that of the Princess. He values status above all, and heeds public opinion in everything he does, concealing or disguising behaviour which might diminish his reputation. We are told that 'il avait toujours conservé des mesures d'honnêteté aux yeux du public et de son domestique', and that when he learns that his wife's infidelity is known to no one, 'cette ignorance entière du public pour son malheur lui fut un adoucissement'. His behaviour thereafter is entirely dependent on his determination to protect his reputation. 'Comme il était l'homme du monde le plus glorieux, il prit le parti qui convenait le mieux à sa gloire et résolut de ne rien laisser voir au public.' That is why he decides not to kill his wife: as he tells her in a letter, his wish to prevent his shame becoming public prevails over his desire for vengeance. He receives the news of the Countess's death with a certain relief because it means that his reputation is no longer under threat. The novel's final sentence, 'Quoiqu'il fût fort jeune, il ne voulut jamais se remarier, et il a vécu jusqu'à un âge fort avancé', indicates his determination never again to allow a wife to jeopardize his public standing.

Navarre follows a much more devious and audacious path. His social status is precarious at the beginning of the story: he has noble birth but no wealth, and his secret wooing of the Princesse de Neufchâtel is designed to remedy this. He deceives throughout, and the ease with which he lies to both the Princess and the Count must cast an element of doubt on his sincerity when he tells the Countess that his love for her has made him indifferent to social advancement: 'il n'est pas question de mon mariage; il ne s'agit plus de ma fortune, il ne s'agit que de votre cœur, madame [. . .]; je renonce à tout le reste' (402). What is certain is that he goes ahead with the exceptionally advantageous marriage that will make his fortune and increase his prestige—'la plus grande et [. . .] la plus agréable fortune où un cadet sans bien eût été jamais élevé' (403). Moreover his deceptions enable him to enjoy the love of both women and maintain his friendship with the Count. Despite this consistent dishonesty his public image is not merely unscathed but greatly enhanced, and he dies in battle with his reputation intact.

Through these three characters, Madame de Lafayette presents us with three very different attitudes to accepted social values. All three are passionate, and all three must find some form of accommodation between their desires and their reputation. Whereas the Count is willing to suffer private humiliation to preserve his public image, the Princess is prepared to endure the public humiliation that results from marrying beneath her. In contrast with them, Navarre plays a daring game of manipulation and deceit to achieve his aims without sacrificing his reputation. Each has to make certain compromises, and each has some measure of success.

But the case of the central character, the one who most engages our interest, is very different. Madame de Lafayette shows the Comtesse de Tende's reluctance to compromise, her difficulty in playing an assumed role, her failure to develop a consistent stratagem, and her consequently disastrous end. Whereas the other characters pursue clearly defined aims—love, reputation, fortune—the Countess drifts from one passionate longing to another, torn between giving precedence to reputation or desire, making and breaking resolutions and creating disorder.

She is little more than a child when she marries the Count and her initial tactics are counterproductive: her outbursts of violent jealousy estrange the husband she passionately loves. When she falls in love with Navarre she is aware of both the private and the public risks she is running and is determined to avoid them, but 'elle tint mal ses résolutions' (401). On the one hand, she is concerned about reputation—her own, that of Navarre and, at the end, that of her husband. Her concern for Navarre's status and prosperity makes her urge him to continue wooing the Princess; and when he comes to see her in secret immediately before his marriage, her thoughts are for both her own reputation and Navarre's public standing: 'Quitter à cause de moi la fortune qui vous attend! je n'en puis seulement supporter la pensée.' On the other hand, her behaviour constantly puts those reputations at risk—'L'on cède aisément à ce qui plaît'—and the element of risk in turn intensifies her passionate behaviour.[8] These two sides of the Comtesse de Tende are very apparent in the scene where her husband discovers Navarre in her bedchamber. With her reputation intact thanks to Navarre's convincing lie, she can appear the obedient wife: 'la comtesse promit de lui dire tout ce que voulait son mari' (406); but at the same time her potential loss of reputation is vividly evoked when the Count condemns Navarre's mistress in terms which unwittingly provide an objective description of his own wife's behaviour: 'Il faut que ce ne soit pas une personne fort estimable de vous aimer et de conserver avec vous un commerce, vous voyant embarqué avec une personne aussi belle que Mme la princesse de Navarre [. . .] Il faut que cette personne n'ait ni esprit, ni courage, ni délicatesse et, en vérité, elle ne mérite pas que vous troubliez un aussi grand bonheur que le vôtre' (406). But although the Countess wants to preserve the reputation of the name of Tende, she can neither renounce her unacceptable passion for Navarre, nor carry out the deception necessary to keep her affair secret. Unable to feign love for her husband, she has rejected his advances, and so when she discovers that she is pregnant there is no possibility of claiming that the child is his. It is only when it is too late that this expedient occurs to her: 'elle conçut quelque légère espérance sur le voyage que son mari devait faire auprès d'elle,

[8] 'Leur passion ne se ralentit pas par les périls et par les obstacles' (404).

et résolut d'en attendre le succès' (408). Although we are told that on hearing of Navarre's death, 'Elle ne craignait plus rien pour son repos, pour sa réputation, ni pour sa vie' (408), she is nevertheless still sufficiently concerned about her reputation to give false reasons to excuse her distress. Despite that concern, however, she cannot bring herself to carry out her plan of seducing her husband and thus hiding her guilty secret for ever. In the end she confesses to him, destroying his view of her as 'la plus estimable femme qu'il eût jamais vue' but at the same time exploiting his ability and determination to preserve public appearances: 'je n'ai pas voulu me déshonorer aux yeux du monde parce que ma réputation vous regarde,' she writes to him; 'conservez-la pour l'amour de vous. Je vais faire paraître l'état où je suis; cachez-en la honte' (410). As the Count admits in his reply, his wish to prevent his shame being publicly known is even stronger than his desire for vengeance; the Countess eventually dies knowing that her public reputation is secure, and begging her husband to expunge the odious private memory of her from his mind.

So the name of Tende appears to be intact—no scandal attaches to it, there is no illegitimate heir and the sullied memory of the Countess is suppressed. To the outside world, the tale of the Comtesse de Tende is a sad but unobjectionable one: she has died in childbirth without leaving an heir to her grieving husband, who never remarries. But privately, the Countess's behaviour has been confused and erratic. She transgresses the social code,[9] but unlike the Princess, she is not willing to face the consequences of her transgression. Neither can she bring herself, like Navarre, to feign and lie in order to protect her reputation. In the end, although she knows that her husband will safeguard her public reputation, she dies of 'la plus violente de toutes les passions' (411)—private shame. Despite the Count's efforts to safeguard the family honour a secret disorder has ensured that the name of Tende will be eliminated. He will never remarry, there is no prospect of an heir, the name cannot pass on.

Indeed, the story itself ends in a final, curious self-suppression since all witnesses to the secret events—the Countess, her baby, her lover and Lalande (their only confident)—have died, and none, we are told, divulged the secret. Only the Countess's confessor and her husband know the truth, and in the terms of the story it is unthinkable

---

[9] When she does decide to embrace 'la vertu' it is much too late (411).

that either would ever reveal it. There is no one left to tell the tale of the Comtesse de Tende: logically, this is a story that cannot be told.

The critics who have interpreted the tale as a profoundly moral one have focused on the discourse of established values which runs through the narrative. Certainly it upholds the virtues of honour, fidelity and honesty; certainly it presupposes the authority of husband over wife and the duty of wife to husband; it assumes that status, merit and wealth go hand in hand. Furthermore, it is a predominantly male discourse which makes implicit appeals to a male reader and evokes shared masculine assumptions. At the end of the first paragraph, for example, we learn that the Count avoids his new wife's company 'et ne vécut plus avec elle *comme l'on vit avec sa femme*' (399). By this use of 'l'on' and 'sa femme', the narrator is clearly appealing to a shared male experience. Similar appeals recur throughout the story, most notably in the account of Tende's reaction when he learns of his wife's infidelity and pregnancy: 'Il pensa d'abord *tout ce qu'il était naturel de penser* en cette occasion; il ne songea qu'à *faire mourir sa femme*' (410). By presenting the Count's reaction to us as perfectly normal and natural, the narrator seems again to invite the reader to consider and judge from a strictly male viewpoint.

And yet that viewpoint is not the only one to find expression. Most readers of novels, after all, were women, and the narrative's blatant appeals to male values may be aimed not at male but at female readers. Read from a female perspective, the expression of male values suddenly seems ironic and disquieting. They are revealed as inappropriate—it cannot be assumed that women readers would readily identify with the male 'l'on', or with the 'natural' desire to murder one's wife. These spurious assertions of 'universal' assumptions merely serve to undermine their own authoritative status, and draw attention instead to the barely expressible alternative which does not give primacy to conventionally received public values.

In his biography of Madame de Lafayette, Roger Duchêne has pieced together enough circumstantial evidence to make a startling hypothesis which seems to corroborate this reading. Bringing together dates, details from letters, scurrilous rumours and the fact that the future Madame de Lafayette was a wealthy heiress who might have been expected to make a better marriage than her very hasty one to an impoverished, widowed provincial aristocrat eighteen years older than herself, Duchêne speculates that she was rushed into the marriage in order to conceal an illegitimate pregnancy.[10] If his theory is correct, the concealed autobiographical element in *La Comtesse de Tende* would account for the text's strangely contradictory nature. It is an untellable tale, simultaneously expressing and suppressing socially inadmissible feelings and behaviour. Repeatedly it returns to questions of secrecy and disclosure as it shows the unbridgeable gulf between honesty and reputation. The double perspective, which at one and the same time expresses and erases a dangerously unconventional perception of women, can plausibly be seen as reflecting the author's own conflicting attitudes. Understandably, perhaps, she did not publish it.

[10] Duchêne, *Madame de Lafayette*, 7–15. Duchêne is careful to point out that although the available facts seem to support his theory, it cannot be proved beyond all doubt. But he puts forward a very plausible case.

CHAPTER 4

❖

La Princesse de Montpensier

The first piece of Madame de Lafayette's fictional writing to be published during her lifetime was *La Princesse de Montpensier*, which appeared anonymously in 1662. At its head is a short note to the reader which carries overtones of the same ambivalence between reticence and revelation that is present in the portrait of Madame de Sévigné and the histories. The note purports to come from the publisher, and states that the story that follows is completely fictitious and has no connection whatsoever with the real Montpensier family. But what appears to be a conventional disclaimer turns out, on closer inspection, to be rather less than innocent. If the story is really no more than 'des aventures inventées à plaisir' as the author claims, why has she—or he (for the author's identity is not revealed)—decided that it is more appropriate to give the characters names from real and eminent families? Why in particular has the author chosen explicitly to evoke the reputation of the real Montpensier Princess while at the same time denying that she and her family have any connection with the 'récit effectivement fabuleux'? And having mentioned Madame de Montpensier by name, why does the disclaimer not refer to other names of distinguished surviving families, such as Anjou and Guise, who also appear in the tale?

For a contemporary reader, this note cannot have failed to bring to mind the most illustrious of the Montpensier women—the Grande Mademoiselle, Anne-Marie d'Orléans, the King's strong-willed cousin, for whose collection of *Portraits* Madame de Lafayette had contributed the piece on Madame de Sévigné. Mademoiselle's political and military involvement in the Fronde had marked the climax of a period of heroic female activity and independence which came to an end with Louis XIV's majority.[1] During Condé's siege of Paris in 1652, she had climbed the ramparts of the Bastille and commanded the troops to turn their cannons and fire on the King's forces. Like

---

[1] See Maclean, 265.

the fictional Princesse de Montpensier, the Grande Mademoiselle was an only daughter and the heiress to a vast fortune; she, too, was manipulated and bargained over (her Memoirs give a colourful and vigorous account of the extraordinary process), but, unable to marry the only man of a rank and distinction she considered appropriate to her own,[2] she refused all the matches that were proposed to her.[3] Her independence of spirit and force of character frequently led her to defy her family's wishes, and whenever the possibility of action arose, she took it. On her return from exile for her part in the Fronde, she went to inspect her ancestral castle at Champigny, near Chinon, and found it virtually rased to the ground. At the time of *La Princesse de Montpensier*'s publication, she was undertaking a major reconstruction of the château de Champigny, in and around which the main incidents of Madame de Lafayette's story take place.[4]

By naming the real Princess in the disclaimer, the author simultaneously evokes and denies the memory of Mademoiselle de Montpensier's courage, strength, independence and endurance. In so doing, she effectively establishes the tone for her story. These assertive qualities are set against the conventional feminine attributes of docility, passivity and obedience. As the plot unfolds, it charts the shifting tensions between the two modes of female conduct. Just as the reference to Catherine de Médicis at the beginning of *La Comtesse de Tende* can be seen as a means of associating the heroine of that story with attributes of independence, authority and disorder, so the fictional Princesse de Montpensier's relationship to the politically assertive Grande Mademoiselle alerts us to a potential female strength. It is unthinkable that Madame de Lafayette should have set out to write a *roman à clef* presenting the Grande Mademoiselle as an adulteress, and there is no question of *La Princesse de Montpensier*'s being read in that way. Yet it cannot be denied that echoes of the Grande

---

[2] Louis XIV, who was referred to as her 'petit mari'.

[3] She twice refused to marry Louis XIV's brother, Philippe, duc d'Anjou, and was exiled for refusing to marry Alfonso VI, King of Portugal. Her disastrous, passionate involvement with Lauzun (whom she may indeed have married in secret) did not begin until several years after the publication of *La Princesse de Montpensier*.

[4] Roger Duchêne records (with some scepticism) Segrais's supposed claim that Mlle de Montpensier was curious to know about the people who had once lived in the ruined castle, and that Madame de Lafayette, as a joke, pretended that *La Princesse de Montpensier* was the transcription of a late sixteenth-century document found among the Montpensier family papers (*Madame de Lafayette*, 206).

Mademoiselle's reputation are felt throughout the tale. It is impossible to read it without being subliminally aware of the historical Princess and therefore of an alternative way of being to that chosen by the fictional Princesse de Montpensier.

It is evident right from the story's opening sentence that love and war are closely linked: 'Pendant que la guerre civile déchirait la France sous le règne de Charles IX, l'Amour ne laissait pas de trouver sa place parmi tant de désordres et d'en causer beaucoup dans son Empire' (5). Love is as devastating as war; both cause disorder and suffering; and both hold total sway over their respective domains. The use of the word 'Empire' here is deliberately ambiguous, playing on both the political sense of a territory ruled, and the *précieux* usage of the attraction with which a woman beguiles her suitor. As the civil war rumbles on in the background, accounts of its progress frequently carry a double meaning, alluding just as easily to the course of courtship as to the course of war. Each is a struggle for domination. Far from being a merely sentimental force, love wields power, rules and destroys, and in describing its operations, Madame de Lafayette will show the male characters using strategies identical to those of warfare. Their aims are those of conquest, as the vocabulary indicates: in love, they wish to *posséder*, *profiter*, *surmonter* and *faire une conquête*.

We are first introduced to the future Princesse de Montpensier as the young heiress Mademoiselle de Mézières, an only child whose wealth and family make her a much-sought-after marriage partner. She is defined solely by her financial and genealogical inheritance; political and dynastic interests determine whom she will marry. At this early stage of the story she is depicted as passive and obedient. Initially presented as little more than merchandise with a very high exchange value,[5] Mademoiselle de Mézières is set in contrast with the men around her, who actively scheme and plot to win her in order to consolidate the power and status of their families. All we learn of her feelings is that 'le duc de Guise [. . .] en fut aimé'. Guise's violently emotional and public reaction to the decision to marry Mademoiselle de Mézières to the Prince de Montpensier contrasts with her own quiet acceptance of the situation: she has internalized

---

[5] e.g. 'la maison de Bourbon, qui ne pouvait voir qu'avec envie l'élévation de celle de Guise, s'apercevant de l'avantage qu'elle recevrait de ce mariage, se résolut de le lui ôter et d'en profiter elle-même en faisant épouser cette héritière au jeune prince de Montpensier' (5).

the moral reasoning which precludes any possibility of continued contact with Guise: 'connaissant par sa vertu qu'il était dangereux d'avoir pour beau-frère un homme qu'elle eût souhaité pour mari, [elle] se résolut enfin de suivre le sentiment de ses proches et conjura M. de Guise de ne plus apporter d'obstacles à son mariage' (6). And so she marries Montpensier.

Immediately after their marriage, Montpensier takes his bride to Champigny to be at a safe distance from Paris which is threatened by the Huguenot army under the command of the Prince de Condé. This historical detail, although authentic, is further evidence that the reputation of the Grande Mademoiselle underlies this text, for it must have reminded contemporary readers of the more recent siege of Paris by the Frondeurs under a later Prince de Condé in 1652. On that occasion Mademoiselle de Montpensier, far from removing herself to a safe distance, had gone to the heart of the fighting. The Prince de Montpensier believes he has removed his bride from danger: Paris is the place 'où *apparemment* tout l'effort de la guerre allait tomber' (6)—but appearances are deceptive. The war to which the text refers is not only a military one. Although the Prince believes that the war centres on Paris and that he has removed his bride to safety, at Champigny the Princess will in fact be involved in another kind of war. The main combatants—Guise, Anjou, Chabanes and Montpensier himself—will all be drawn there, and it is there that the final 'battle' will take place. Try as he will, Montpensier cannot remove his wife from danger; since she is the prize being fought over, the 'war' will follow her wherever she goes.

So when the Huguenots later besiege Poitiers, and Montpensier moves his wife back to Paris 'pour n'être plus si proche des lieux où se faisait la guerre', he is paradoxically moving her to a yet more exposed position. In Paris, 'Le duc d'Anjou ne changea pas . . . les sentiments qu'il avait conçus pour elle à Champigny', and 'Le duc de Guise acheva d'en devenir violemment amoureux' (14–15).

Even when Montpensier leaves his bride in safety, as he thinks, at Champigny, in the care of his old and trusted friend the Comte de Chabanes, Chabanes proceeds to fall in love with her. When we read that Chabanes, unlike most lovers, does not try to create disharmony between husband and wife, the picture of marital harmony is immediately undermined by a comment which is ostensibly about the course of the war: 'La paix ne fit que paraître.' The apparent tranquillity of the Montpensier household is indeed short-lived. A few lines later we read of the Princess's distress at 'les périls où la guerre allait exposer son mari'—again, for 'guerre' we may substitute 'passion'.

The joint allusions to love and war intensify as the story nears its end. A reference to the preparations for the massacre of St Bartholomew's Day (25) creates a sense of impending doom which is not restricted to the fortunes of the war; these preparations are directly responsible for the gathering of Chabanes, Guise and Montpensier at Champigny. And the description of the final crisis which ensues from that confrontation conveys a vivid visual impression of an 'horrible massacre' (32), as Montpensier collapses on a bed, Chabanes slumps against a table, and the Princess falls senseless to the floor.

Initially, as the struggle unfolds, it seems that the Princess will play the conventional female role of obedient passivity, watching from the sidelines as the men engage in wars on both fronts. When we are first introduced to her as Mademoiselle de Mézières she appears silent, pliant and consenting, a model of the womanly virtues much praised by writers of the period. In contrast to her docility, the men who wish to marry her are shown as active, passionate and forceful. But as the story progresses, the behaviour conventionally expected of both sexes begins to be called into question. Nowhere are sexual stereotypes more clearly challenged than in the character of the Comte de Chabanes. His sexuality is ambiguous: passionately devoted to the Prince de Montpensier, he also falls in love with the Princess. Indeed, he becomes a focus for the ambiguities of the text. Unlike the other male characters, who are militarily active, he remains largely detached from the movements of the war. At the outset of the story he has Huguenot sympathies and great prospects under Condé, but declares himself for the Catholic side because of his devotion to Montpensier. Yet he is eventually murdered as a Huguenot in the St Bartholomew's Day massacre. And his ambivalent religious, political and sexual leanings are echoed in his ambivalent morality. His integrity is repeatedly compromised in spite of his highly principled utterances. So when the Prince de Montpensier departs for the war, leaving his bride at Champigny with Chabanes, she comes under the influence of a man whose moral identity and principles are far from certain. She is described at this stage as though incomplete, unformed, waiting to be moulded into perfection by Chabanes: 'Se servant de l'amitié qu'elle lui témoignait, pour lui inspirer des sentiments d'une vertu extraordinaire et digne de la grandeur de sa naissance, il la rendit en peu de temps une des personnes du monde la plus achevée' (7).

But Chabanes is the least fitting person to undertake such a task. Emblematic of the moral, behavioural and sexual ambiguities that run through the story, his own ambivalence repeatedly leads to disastrous consequences. He frequently makes resolutions which he immediately breaks, and his inability to choose and play out a consistent role is a trigger for his and the Princesse de Montpensier's downfall. The social manœuvring described in this story is complex and ruthless, and it is clear that Chabanes is disastrously ineffectual. Even his angry letter of 'éternel adieu' to the Princess has little meaning, for he soon rushes to see her again and is immediately 'plus soumis qu'il n'avait jamais été' (25). Rejected as a suitor by the Princess, yet rejected by the Prince under suspicion of being the Princess's lover; ignored by the Princess and Guise alike;[6] altruistically planning the midnight rendezvous between the Princess and Guise which betrays all of them; declaring himself for the Catholic side yet being killed as a Huguenot—Chabanes is defeated in both love and war without ever having fully committed himself to either.

The men who behave more conventionally use a variety of tactics which quickly change from outright mutual confrontation (at the beginning of the tale) to a more subtle play of stealth and pursuit. Gradually, they close in on the Princess. We first see this procedure at work when the Princess is in a small boat moored in the centre of the river, with Anjou, Guise and their retinue on the bank. Like the women in the *Mémoires de la cour de France*, the Princess is physically confined in a small space and has little freedom of movement, while the men are able to range freely through the countryside. Once she has been told that the strangers on the river bank are the King's brother, the Duc d'Anjou and his followers, she has no alternative but to engage with them and bring them to Champigny. The second episode comes at the end of the novel: once again, the Princess is in a confined space—in her chamber in the château de Champigny, ringed around by protective walls and moats. One by one the defences are broken down: Guise and Chabanes enter the park, 'et, passant par des brèches qui étaient aux murailles, ils vinrent dans le

---

[6] e.g. 'Ce duc [de Guise], occupé de son dessein, ne prit non plus garde à l'embarras du comte que la princesse de Montpensier avait fait à son silence lorsqu'elle lui avait conté son amour' (26).

parterre'. Then they cross the lowered drawbridge which leads directly to the Princess's anteroom, and pass on into the inner chamber and the final dénouement.

In both cases the Princess sits quietly and waits, while her suitors are active and mobile. Yet her inactivity is not passive. In the episode by the river, she explains that she had left Champigny with her husband, intending to follow him in the hunt, but instead came to see a salmon being caught in a net. She 'regardait avec attention deux hommes qui pêchaient auprès d'elle'. At this point in the heavily symbolic and self-reflexive passage, whose literary contrivance is stressed by the comment that the Princess 'parut une chose de roman', we are invited to see her as a mere spectator of her own fate, watching the two fishermen/suitors trying to lure and catch their prey. Their tactics are those of battle: orders are given, a group of horsemen advance through the water, and finally Guise and Anjou board the little boat. But at this stage a different reading is offered, in which the Princess plays the active part. She has chosen to leave her husband to hunt on his own, and is instead out to ensnare her own quarry. No longer metaphorically represented by the fish, the Princess now becomes the fisherman who is about to catch the salmon Guise in her net. As she relates that the salmon 'avait donné dans un filet', Guise realizes that 'il sortirait difficilement de cette aventure sans rentrer dans ses liens' (11). Here is the same contradiction and tension that we have encountered before: the events say one thing (the Princess, quiet, cool, obedient, is forced to meet Guise by a chance encounter with the King's brother), but the sub-text says another (the Princess is active; she chooses to leave her husband and go to pursue her own quarry; it is she who invites the two dukes into her boat). Her apparent passivity is highly deceptive, for she has the power of a fatal attraction, and even to set eyes on her could be perilous. As Anjou remarks a few pages later: 'sa vue lui pourrait être dangereuse, s'il y était souvent exposé' (13).

By the middle of the tale, the Princess is in a position of total command. Her power over Guise is even greater than that of the King himself. 'Vous serez satisfaite, Madame [. . .] Je m'en vais faire pour vous ce que toute la puissance royale n'aurait pu obtenir de moi. Il m'en coûtera ma fortune, mais c'est peu de chose pour vous satisfaire' (21). Guise's plan is to marry the Princesse de Portien in order to allay the Princesse de Montpensier's suspicion that he has turned his affections to the sister of the Duc d'Anjou, and at the same time to prevent public speculation about his interest in the Princesse de Montpensier. When news of this marriage becomes public, the Princesse de Montpensier is overjoyed, and 'elle fut bien aise de voir par là le pouvoir qu'elle avait sur le duc de Guise' (21).

But, paradoxically, by exercising this power she has made herself all the more vulnerable. By marrying beneath him, Guise has regained the upper hand for his sacrifice obliges the Princess to yield to him: 'Cette belle princesse ne put refuser son cœur à un homme qui l'avait possédé autrefois et qui venait de tout abandonner pour elle. Elle consentit donc à recevoir ses voeux' (22).

From this point of surrender, the Princess's vulnerability can only increase. She cannot resist Guise, and she must obey her husband's peremptory commands: 'Le prince de Montpensier [. . .] ordonna à la princesse sa femme de s'en aller à Champigny. Ce commandement lui fut bien rude; il fallait pourtant obéir' (23). Even Chabanes begins to resist her influence, and the Princess now regrets having 'si peu ménagé un homme sur qui elle avait tant de pouvoir'. But Chabanes is weak, for 'l'on est bien faible quand on est amoureux'—another double-edged comment which ostensibly refers to Chabanes, but which comes just as the Princess's own position is at its most vulnerable; he is persuaded to return to her service, and gives the help and advice which lead to the final disaster.

When Chabanes tells the Princesse de Montpensier that Guise is in the area and wishes to see her, she finds herself 'dans une extrémité épouvantable'. From then on she is described as weak, without a will of her own, utterly in Guise's thrall: 'elle fut quelque temps sans revenir à elle'; 'elle n'en eut pas la force'; 'elle ne put résister davantage'. Her defeat is now complete. The only emotion she is described as feeling when Guise arrives is one of shame, and she remains in a state of complete collapse for the rest of the story—fainting on the floor, collapsing at her husband's feet, lying mortally ill in bed, and succumbing to the *coup de grâce* of hearing of Guise's unfaithfulness.

This identification of love with war, and the perception of relationships between men and women as struggles for mastery ending in victory or defeat, are a transposition into fiction of those same patterns which Madame de Lafayette describes in her histories of life at the French court. In this particular 'war' the Princesse de Montpensier's initial position of strength has gradually been eroded. Her power has waned, and when she finally realizes this, she dies.

The last few lines hint again at the double perspective evoked by the story's ambiguous title: 'Elle mourut en peu de jours, dans la fleur de son âge, une des plus belles princesses du monde, et qui aurait été sans doute la plus heureuse, si la vertu et la prudence eussent conduit toutes ses actions' (33). Ostensibly a moralizing conclusion, it nevertheless runs counter to a comment that comes immediately before, and highlights the ambiguity of Madame de Lafayette's portrayal of her women characters. What has caused the Princess's final agony is her discovery that Guise has transferred his affections to the Marquise de Noirmoutier. Unlike his feelings for the Princess, his love for the Marquise is not only intense but enduring: 'il s'y attacha entièrement et l'aima avec une passion démesurée et qui lui dura jusques à sa mort' (32). The Marquise de Noirmoutier has inspired the kind of lasting devotion which all Madame de Lafayette's heroines seek but never find. We are not told much about the Marquise, but what little is revealed throws light on the final judgement on the Princesse de Montpensier. Both women are witty and beautiful, but the Marquise 'était une personne qui prenait autant de soin de faire éclater ses galanteries que les autres en prennent de les cacher' (33). In other words, she is someone whose behaviour is antithetical to that of the Princess. She does not possess the 'virtues' of self-restraint, discretion and prudent silence; she delights in displaying her love-affairs; and consequently, it is suggested, she inspires in Guise a passion of a kind that he never felt for the Princess. We are told that the Princess would have been the happiest person in the world if only she had behaved in a more prudent and virtuous fashion, and yet the Marquise de Noirmoutier, by being neither prudent nor virtuous, by adopting that confident, vigorous and outspoken mode implicit in the parallels with the Grande Mademoiselle which contemporaries might have drawn from the story's title, lives happily ever after.

CHAPTER 5

❖

Zaïde

Zaïde, histoire espagnole was first published in 1669 as the work of Jean de Segrais, secretary to Mademoiselle de Montpensier and friend of Madame de Lafayette.[1] Its complex structure and stylized narratives, very different from the simplicity of Madame de Lafayette's other works, derive from a tradition of pastoral and lyrical love-romances that stretches back to *L'Astrée*. Set in ninth-century Spain, it takes as its narrative core the relationship between Consalve, Prince of Castille, and a Moorish princess, Zaïde.

Madame de Lafayette uses a series of interpolated stories, letters and monologues to explore the circumstances of the main characters, to contrast the predicaments of one with another, and to create suspense by delaying the final resolution of all the impediments which stand

---

[1] For some time *Zaïde* was believed to be solely Segrais's work, and he himself referred to it as 'ma *Zaïde*', but he made it clear in his memoirs that although it appeared under his name, Madame de Lafayette was the principal author. His contribution, he says, was limited to advice on the novel's structure: 'Zaïde, qui a paru sous mon nom est aussi d'elle. Il est vrai que j'en ai eu quelque part, mais seulement pour la disposition du roman, où les règles de l'art sont observées avec grande exactitude.' La Rochefoucauld and Pierre-Daniel Huet seem also to have had a part in the novel's creation. The Bibliothèque Nationale owns a page of *Zaïde* in La Rochefoucauld's handwriting, and some critics believe that he may have made suggestions about the psychology of the characters. The scholar and philosopher Huet was asked by Madame de Lafayette to correct the style of *Zaïde*, and he also provided the novel with a preface in the form of his treatise *De l'origine des romans*.

It is clear that *Zaïde* was the result of some form of collaboration between Madame de Lafayette and more experienced men of letters, but it is impossible to be sure about the nature and extent of each contribution. It seems likely that Madame de Lafayette discussed the plans and progress of her work with Segrais, Huet and La Rochefoucauld, and sought from them advice on details of structure, style and convention; and they may have corrected or modified some passages. In spite of the absence of her name from the original title-page, it is now generally agreed that Madame de Lafayette deserves to be considered as the novel's main author. Modern editions invariably have her name alone on the cover, with Segrais's contribution relegated to a footnote if mentioned at all. Yet the precise extent of her authorship remains in question.

between Consalve and Zaïde. Less than half the novel is devoted to the principal story, which unfolds over the space of one year as convention demanded.[2] The remainder is taken up with tales of Consalve's past (his changing fortunes at court and his previous love affair with Nugna Bella who betrays him with one of his closest friends, Don Ramire); the story of Alphonse, Consalve's companion in exile, who loves and is loved by Bélasire, but who destroys their relationship by his obsessive jealousy; the tale of Consalve's sister, Hermenesilde, and her marriage to Don Garcie who usurps his father as King of Léon; the long and involved recounting of the numerous love affairs of Alamir, Prince of Tharse, which precede his unrequited passion for Zaïde; and an account of the lives of Zaïde and her companion Félime before the shipwreck with which these ramified stories begin.

Even a century after the novel's publication it was still greatly admired as a pleasant, well-constructed tale with a sound moral. In 1774, for example, Sabatiers de Castres wrote that '*Zaïde* est un des meilleurs Romans. Le plan en est bien concerté, les passions en sont sages, les détails agréables, le dénouement très heureux.'[3] Yet despite the novel's conventional structure and its seemingly balanced presentation of a variety of different attitudes to love, Madame de Lafayette's authorship of *Zaïde* is confirmed by the way in which it explores many of the problems of women's role and women's voice which clearly preoccupy her.

One question on which *La Comtesse de Tende* and *La Princesse de Montpensier* merely touched, and which figures quietly in all Madame de Lafayette's work, is confronted in *Zaïde* with extraordinary boldness. It is the problem of communication between the sexes. In *Zaïde* this becomes the central focus, the driving force behind the narrative. It is introduced at the beginning of the novel when Consalve is walking by the seashore and discovers the seemingly lifeless body of a young woman whose name, he later discovers, is Zaïde. She regains consciousness the following day, but neither she nor Consalve is able to speak: 'Consalve ne pouvait exprimer par ses paroles l'admiration qu'il avait pour elle' (44), and 'la parole ne revenait point à cette

---

[2] See Roger Francillon, *L'Œuvre romanesque de Madame de Lafayette* (Paris: Corti, 1973), 66 and ch.1 part III.

[3] M. l'Abbé S*** de Castres, *Les Trois Siècles de la littérature française*, 5th edn. (La Haye: 1781), ii. 267.

étrangère. [. . .] la nuit et le jour suivant se passèrent sans qu'elle prononçât une seule parole' (44). When she does eventually begin to talk, it is in a language that Consalve cannot understand. He tries to speak to her in Arabic, Spanish and Italian, but is met with incomprehension. She continues to address him in her own language, pausing 'comme pour attendre qu'on lui répondît' (45). But Consalve cannot reply in terms that she can understand, and this extraordinary passage ends with both characters in a state of anxiety and anguish, isolated from one another by their inability to communicate.

As the narrative continues, it becomes clear that this mutual incomprehension is caused by something much more far-reaching than a mere foreign-language barrier. Zaïde mysteriously disappears and Consalve, despairing of ever finding her again, sets off for Italy. He spends the first night of his journey in Tortosa, wandering sadly along the river bank in the dark, when he overhears a woman speaking Spanish in a nearby garden. The timbre of her voice reminds him of Zaïde. Fragments of what she says are clearly audible, yet Consalve pays little attention because he 'knows' that Zaïde cannot speak Spanish (129–30). Without realizing it, he is in fact listening to her voice speaking his own language, but the mental barrier between them remains as impenetrable as the darkness which hides her from his sight and prevents him from recognizing her. The point is further stressed on the following day, when he sees Zaïde on board a ship on the river but decides not to communicate with her until her vessel has berthed. This time he knows that he has found his beloved, he knows that he can now speak her language and she his, and yet the distance between them still cannot be bridged. Consalve is arrested and taken prisoner on the river bank while Zaïde, oblivious to his presence, is carried on downstream. Consalve's lament is an eloquent statement of the impossibility of communication between them:

Quelle destinée que la mienne! dit-il en lui-même. Je perds Zaïde dans le même moment que je la retrouve! Quand je la voyais et que je lui parlais dans la maison d'Alphonse, elle ne pouvait m'entendre. Lorsque je l'ai rencontrée à Tortose et que j'en pouvais être entendu, je ne l'ai pas reconnue; et maintenant que je la vois, que je la reconnais et qu'elle pourrait m'entendre, je ne saurais lui parler et je n'espère plus de la revoir. (133)

Much later in the novel, when he and Zaïde do finally meet in the castle of Talavera, no obvious linguistic barrier remains. Yet they still fail to understand one another. They start to speak simultaneously, each using the other's language, and so the resultant 'exchange' is as incomprehensible to them as the clash of languages at the beginning of their story. Then, in their astonishment at hearing their own language in the mouth of the other, both are dumbstruck and remain in a 'profond silence' for some time. The sudden realization that communication is at least theoretically possible is not entirely welcome. Consalve admits as much to Zaïde: 'Je ne sais, madame, [. . .] si j'ai eu raison de souhaiter, autant que je l'ai fait, que vous me puissiez entendre; peut-être n'en serai-je pas moins malheureux'; Zaïde listens to this with embarrassment, and thereafter reverts to her mother tongue (144).[4] As a subsequent exchange between the couple makes clear, the difficulty they have in understanding one another stems from an impediment more fundamental than a simply linguistic one: 'Je ne sais, madame, répondit Consalve, si ce que vous me dites m'est favorable et je ne puis vous en rendre grâce si vous ne me l'expliquez mieux. Je vous en ai trop dit pour vous l'expliquer, répliqua Zaïde [. . .] Je suis bien destiné au malheur de ne vous pas entendre, reprit Consalve, puisque, même en me parlant espagnol, je ne sais ce que vous me dites' (146). The hero and heroine cannot understand one another either literally or in the broader sense: their mutual incomprehension even when they appear to speak the same language dramatizes the fundamental problem of communication between the sexes.

Their inability to understand one another contrasts with the ease and openness with which each communicates with members of the same sex. Much is made of the bond that develops between Alphonse and Consalve as they exchange confidences, and the ease with which Zaïde and Félime communicate emphasizes the mutual incomprehension that exists between Zaïde and Consalve.[5]

On a superficial reading, the communication problems of this couple act as a rather implausible device for prolonging suspense and adding to the obstacles which the lovers must overcome before they

---

[4] Cf. Alphonse's fear that if he can overcome Bélasire's doubts and persuade her of his love and be loved by her in return, he will be 'exposé au malheur de cesser d'être aimé' (110). He believes that love depends on uncertainty about the true feelings of the other.

[5] See 42 and 45. Cf. also the inability of Don Garcie's officer to understand the women on whom he is trying to eavesdrop: 'Elles parlaient assez haut, mais je n'entendais pas ce qu'elles disaient, parce qu'elles parlaient une langue que je ne connais point et qui n'est pas celle des Arabes' (156).

can finally be united in the conventional happy ending. But such a reading leaves unanswered the question of why Madame de Lafayette should choose this particular form of obstacle rather than another. It also fails to confront the fact that it is an obstacle which is never finally resolved—the misunderstandings and inarticulacy continue until the last page of the novel. The happy ending, therefore, must be seen as an ironic one. There is nothing to suggest that the jealousy, anguish and despair that have arisen from the inability of Zaïde and Consalve to communicate with one another will suddenly end with their marriage.[6] The communication problem that exists between them is not simply a linguistic hurdle to be overcome by practice—it is a metaphorical representation of a generalized and insoluble problem of communication between men and women.

Other couples within the novel experience different but equally insoluble difficulties of mutual comprehension. Whereas Consalve and Zaïde are literally unable to communicate for much of the plot, Alphonse and Bélasire talk freely to one another. But although Bélasire replies openly to all the questions Alphonse asks about her feelings for her previous suitors, the distance between the two is as great as that between Consalve and Zaïde. This is because Alphonse is incapable of reacting to what he hears. No number of assurances of love and faithfulness from Bélasire can stem his obsessive jealousy. Similarly, Alamir's repeated tests of his devoted lover Elsibery fail to satisfy him, and nothing she says or does can convince him of her constancy: 'ce redoublement d'amour lui parut une infidélité et lui causa le même chagrin que la diminution lui en aurait dû causer' (197). Each of these men remains deaf to what he hears from the object of his desire: regardless of what the woman says or does, he distorts the message to fit it into his preconceived view of things.

Yet it is important to note that in every case, it is the man who is presented as mistaken. In some sense the women are repositories of truth—the reader has more faith in their judgements and expressions of emotion, while distrusting the outpourings of the male characters.[7] Most of the women express their thoughts and feelings honestly, if

[6] Roger Francillon sees the incongruously happy ending following on from the novel's pessimistic presentation of love as a concession to the demands of the genre. In his view it constitutes a major flaw which explains why the novel has not stood the test of time (*L'Œuvre romanesque*, 66).

[7] The female characters are distrustful too. Bélasire, for example, 'avait une défiance naturelle de tous les hommes' (109).

reticently. It is the men who ignore or misperceive the message, and their behaviour is shown to be mistaken to the point of perversity. Even Consalve's unfaithful first love, Nugna Bella, whose deceitfulness might seem an exception to this presentation of female truth, is shown to have a far shrewder understanding of the world than does Consalve. With her, too, Consalve repeatedly mistakes or ignores the evidence: 'On ne connaît point les femmes', he despairingly concludes, adding, less convincingly, and as if to console himself, 'elles ne se connaissent pas elles-mêmes' (84).

But perhaps the most extraordinary feature of the novel's exploration of the problems of communication between men and women is the response of critics to it. Most simply ignore it. Those few who do pass comment tend to dismiss it as an artificial device lacking in credibility. When the novel first appeared, Bussy-Rabutin complained that the way in which Consalve falls in love with Zaïde at first sight, and without understanding her language, was utterly implausible:

Tout cela m'a paru hors de la vraisemblance, et je ne puis souffrir que le héros du roman fasse le personnage d'un fou. Si c'était une histoire, il faudrait supprimer ce qui n'est pas vraisemblable, car les choses extraordinaires qui choquent le bon sens discréditent les vérités. Mais dans un roman où l'on est maître des événements, il les faut rendre croyables, et qu'au moins le héros ne fasse pas des extravagances.[8]

It is unacceptable to Bussy-Rabutin that the hero of a novel should be depicted as a fool, and he rejects Consalve's behaviour as implausible. He is totally blind to the female perspective from which Madame de Lafayette is writing, and he speaks for subsequent critics when he dismisses these extraordinary twists of plot as being so implausible as to 'discredit the truth'. Yet their very excess commands our attention. To object to the plot's language barriers because they seem improbable, or to ignore them, as critics have done, even though they constitute the dominant structuring force of the novel, is to dismiss a problem of the relations between the sexes which runs through Madame de Lafayette's entire work.

Essentially, *Zaïde* is an exploration of different perceptions of the nature of love, and of the difficulties in recognizing, describing or explaining a passion which constantly eludes reason. Initially confident characters are reduced to a state of bewilderment as feelings

---

[8] *Lettres*, ed. Lalanne (Paris, 1858), i. 241–2, cit. Laugaa, 13.

and events spin out of control, and much of the plot consists of their attempts to fight this sense of perplexity. The structure of the novel itself underscores the tension between control and confusion: the complicated network of characters, emotions and events is presented in a series of parallel or contrasting tales which offer alternative perspectives but from which no ultimate truth or moral ever emerges. *Zaïde* resists prescriptive and reductive interpretations.

Yet one clear focus is the sharp distinction between the behaviour, values and assumptions of the male and female characters. Whereas *La Princesse de Montpensier* and the *Mémoires* do little more than hint at the unwelcome physical limitations on women's lives, *Zaïde* makes far more explicit reference to the restrictions faced by the Spanish and Arab women. Consalve and Nugna Bella complain of 'la manière retirée dont les femmes sont obligées de vivre en Espagne' (57), while the Arab women have even less freedom, living under 'cette contrainte insupportable' (182).[9] The exotic setting permits the use of extreme examples of these restrictions: women are half-hidden behind screens or windows, concealed behind walls, glimpsed through veils, and closely guarded. But the most serious restrictions they face lie much deeper, as the story of Zabelec shows.

Zabelec seems initially to have burst free from the usual female constraints—she refuses to marry the wealthy man chosen by her parents, marries her lover instead, and runs away from home, dressed as a man, to follow him to sea. But after being betrayed and abandoned by him, she chooses to live in her friend Elsibery's household disguised as a male slave. Full of cautions to Elsibery to avoid suffering a similar 'horrible infidélité' (198), Zabelec nevertheless still loves her husband passionately and constantly hopes for his return. She remains as a slave, despite Elsibery's father's frequent offers to set her free, until she learns of her husband's death. Zabelec is, in other words, literally a slave to passion. When she dresses and acts as a slave, she is merely giving a visual representation to her wretched and powerless condition, prior to her ultimate and total withdrawal from the world.

Her story comes immediately after Sélémin has told Elsibery that marriage is the only escape from 'cette captivité éternelle' to which single women are condemned (194). Marriage is proposed to Elsibery as the only escape from perpetual imprisonment; yet her friend Zabelec marries and is enslaved. For the women there is no escape

[9] See further examples, 175 and 185.

and no alternative. Zabelec's unconventional behaviour—her rejection of her parents' choice of husband, her elopement, her adoption of male disguises, her cynical warnings to Elsibery—cannot liberate her. And even after her husband's infidelity, betrayal, desertion and death, when she has no more external reasons for hiding, she emerges from her disguise only to withdraw, with Elsibery, into total isolation: the two women go to live 'éloignée[s] du commerce de tous les hommes [. . .] dans un profond oubli de tous les attachements de la terre' (198), prefiguring the final withdrawal of the Princesse de Clèves.

When women such as Zabelec and Elsibery (and other women abandoned by Alamir) decide to withdraw from the world, their retreat is final, and of a very different nature from that of male characters. Consalve, Alphonse and Alamir all withdraw into solitude or disguise at some point. Indeed, the work opens with Consalve deciding to leave Spain in order to 'se retirer dans quelque solitude' (38). But in each of these cases the narrative follows the retreating or disguised man. The textual abandonment of Alamir's discarded lovers, the death of Félime, the retreat of Elsibery and Zabelec all reinforce the impression that the narrative is following a male perspective. It is as if the women are of interest only in so far as they are love-objects. Consalve may have left the court, but the novel's centre of interest moves away from the court with him and focuses on his subsequent adventures. Unlike Zabelec, when Alamir adopts a disguise he does so in order to give himself extra room for action.

Madame de Lafayette portrays the men as searching for control—control of their feelings, of their surroundings, of their State, of their lives. Their quest for control frequently takes the form of a search for knowledge and certainty. They treat knowledge as something objective, separate from the knower, something which can be mastered. And yet such mastery generally proves to be illusory. The women, on the other hand, appear not to attach importance to that kind of knowledge; they operate in a different, more instinctive mode.

The principal area where we find the male characters attempting to gain control is the sphere of love. They see passion as dangerous and menacing, and love as a battleground where they are threatened by the 'dangereux pouvoir des femmes' (83), but they believe that love will lose its menace if they can fully understand it. Time and again, the men elaborate a theory of love starting from first principles; time and again they are proved wrong. The theory does not correspond to lived reality, and it is repeatedly shown that passions cannot be predicted or controlled.

From an early stage in the novel we find hints that Consalve is an unreliable theoretician of love. Watching Zaïde and Félime's behaviour after he has rescued them from drowning—Zaïde weeping, Félime apparently trying to console her—he elaborates the hypothesis that Zaïde was shipwrecked while following her lover, whose death she is now mourning, 'et, enfin, il crut savoir comme s'il l'eût appris d'elle-même, que l'amour était la cause de ses pleurs' (48). Consalve's conviction that he has correctly interpreted Zaïde's tears is ironically contrasted with his inability to understand his own responses. His surge of jealousy for Zaïde's imagined lover is not only an emotion he has never before experienced, but one which astonishes him with its intensity: 'Cette passion, qui lui était inconnue, se fit sentir en lui, pour la première fois, avec tant de violence qu'il crut être frappé de quelque douleur que les autres hommes ne connaissent point' (48). The irony of his misapprehension becomes even more apparent when he tries to verify his suspicion. He asks Zaïde why she is so distressed, knowing full well that he will not receive an answer since she can neither understand what he is saying to her, nor explain herself to him: 'assuré qu'elle ne lui pouvait répondre, il ne laissa pas de le lui demander. Elle était bien éloignée de comprendre ce qu'il lui voulait dire' (48). She cannot explain to him because his question is incomprehensible to her—and for reasons that are more than simply linguistic.

We subsequently discover that this is not the first time that Consalve has been mistaken about love. Before he had ever experienced love, he had elaborated a number of theories about it: that he could never fall in love with a woman who had already been in love with another man; that love at first sight was an impossibility; that a man can fall in love with a woman only if he knows her well and has grown to respect her—theories which are of course undermined by Consalve's experience of an immediate and unreasoned passion for Zaïde, as well as by the bitter outcome of his affair with Nugna Bella whom he knew well and yet misjudged.

Alphonse's theories about love are just as strongly asserted, and prove to be just as untenable. He maintains that jealousy is a sure sign of love. His own intense but groundless jealousy, however, is destructive of love, causing the death of his innocent friend Don Manrique and the loss of his beloved Bélasire, who enters a convent. From his initial delight at seeing Bélasire lose control over her feelings—'Quel charme c'était pour moi de connaître l'étonnement qu'avait Bélasire de n'être plus maîtresse d'elle-même et de se trouver des sentiments sur quoi elle n'avait point de pouvoir!' (109)—Alphonse proceeds to lose control over his own. 'Folie', 'fureur', 'désespoir' and 'rage' are the words he uses in retrospect to describe the torments of his unfounded jealousy. Moreover, Alphonse has had every opportunity to discover Bélasire's true nature. Unlike Consalve, he has had long and open conversations with the object of his passion, as he explains: 'nous parlâmes ensemble avec un air plus libre qu'apparemment nous ne le devions avoir dans une première conversation' (107). Yet he completely misjudges her character.

Don Garcie, Prince of Léon, has a happier experience of love, but he, too, is forced to abandon his initial theory. He starts from the premiss that men fall in love with beautiful women whom they do not know; he argues that he would be incapable of loving a woman to whom he had become accustomed. For this reason Consalve wants to introduce his sister, Hermenesilde, to Don Garcie. Hermenesilde is still very young and has not yet reached the height of her beauty: according to this theory Don Garcie will not try to seduce her when she is older, because she will be too familiar to him. But again, theory is proved wrong: Don Garcie does fall in love with Hermenesilde, and the theory is more triumphantly overturned when he marries her and makes her his Queen.

Alamir, Prince of Tharse, also finds his attitude to love overturned during the course of the novel. Initially, he is presented as a man who is loved by many but who is incapable of passion: his pleasure comes from the difficulties and 'mystères' of the chase, and as soon as he is satisfied that he is truly loved in return, he loses interest. But when he meets Zaïde he falls helplessly in love. As he says, 'Je n'ai pas pu aimer toutes celles qui m'ont aimé : Zaïde me méprise et je l'adore' (199). So, although he had believed that obstacles to love were his true source of pleasure, when faced with the ultimate obstacle—Zaïde's continued indifference to him—he finds only anguish and finally death.

In each of these cases the man starts off with a belief about the nature of his response to love, and in each case his belief turns out to be mistaken. The men's views on love are based on unreal images of women rather than on direct observation or experience. Madame de Lafayette's narrative follows these male fantasies and gradually reveals their inadequacy.

Nowhere is this more obvious than in the case of Zaïde. Her central importance is stressed by the novel's title, and it is she who provides the narrative focus, the goal that has to be attained before the novel can end. Yet her presence in the text is minimal—she remains a hidden, silent, enigmatic figure, a figment of Consalve's imagination. Her first appearance is as a mere object—a mysterious, shapeless, glittering mass washed up on the seashore to be discovered and brought to life by the hero: 'Le soleil . . . fit briller à ses yeux quelque chose d'éclatant qu'il ne put distinguer d'abord et qui lui donna seulement la curiosité de s'en approcher' (43). Gradually this limp, inert form is revived, but she remains nameless (referred to as 'cette inconnue', or 'cette étrangère') for some time, and is absent for much of the novel. Consalve determinedly pursues Zaïde but does not understand her even in the most basic sense. A detail in Félime's account towards the end of the novel offers a glimpse of a Zaïde very different from this passive, silent, mourning creature of Consalve's fantasy. Félime describes their initial encounter with Alamir, who is sailing to shore as she and Zaïde sail out. Although both women recognize the impropriety of showing their interest in the handsome stranger and his retinue, Zaïde delights in having their boat go through unexpected manœuvres to discover whether Alamir's vessel will still follow. Far from being reticent or inactive, the Zaïde that emerges from Félime's account is an adventurous, seductive and independent woman who revels in the admiration of a handsome stranger.

That side of Zaïde is only hinted at, however. The central figure, the name of the title, remains an enigma, largely absent from the narrative or silent in it, and her apparent effacement is repeated in the presentation of the other female characters. They too appear only as a function of male desire, and remain shadowy figures because they are essentially male fantasies. They disappear from the pages of the book as soon as they cease to be objects of pursuit. Even Félime follows this pattern, although she is not loved by a man and is not an object of pursuit, for her role in the novel is totally dependent on her unrequited and unspoken passion for Alamir: she survives his death by only twenty-four hours. The sense of 'self' projected by the female characters is so tenuous that it vanishes if not supported by a man. There seems to be no way, in this novel, in which a woman can exist without a husband or suitor. Retreat or death are the only alternatives.[10]

[10] It is possible that this underlying male perspective stems from one or more of Madame de Lafayette's male collaborators. See above, n. 1.

The sad tale of Félime offers Madame de Lafayette the opportunity to explore another aspect of a problem which runs like a leitmotif through her work: the benefits and dangers of silence. Already present as a theme in her portrait of Madame de Sévigné, and developed further in *La Comtesse de Tende*, the *Histoire de Madame* and *La Princesse de Clèves*, it is clearly a subject which fascinates and preoccupies her, and which has an important bearing on her own choice of anonymous authorship. In *Zaïde* the issue is explored with characteristic subtlety. Unlike the male characters, who readily and lengthily declare their emotions, the female characters are reticent and wary. Conventions of polite behaviour of course demanded that women hide their feelings of love—as Félime explains: 'je le [Alamir] vis pour elle [Zaïde] comme j'eusse été pour lui, si la bienséance m'eût permis de faire voir mes sentiments' (171). But Félime chooses not to talk of her passion for Alamir because she fears that doing so would make her vulnerable to betrayal. As she laments after Alamir's death: 'Ah! pourquoi lui ai-je si soigneusement caché la passion que j'avais pour lui! [. . .] Que craignais-je? Pourquoi ne voulais-je pas qu'il sût que je l'adorais? [. . .] Hé bien! quand il l'aurait su, il aurait feint de m'aimer et m'aurait trompé (229).[11] She believes that in silence lies self-protection, and her story is that of her struggle with silence. Her first breach of the silence occurs when she overcomes 'tous les mouvements d'orgueil et de honte' and tearfully confesses to Zaïde her love for Alamir. Zaïde's reaction is one of surprise—not because Félime loves Alamir, but because she has not told him so: 'Mais pourquoi [. . .] avez-vous caché si soigneusement vos sentiments à celui qui les a fait naître?' she asks. 'Je ne doute point que, s'il les avait découverts d'abord, il ne vous eût aimée; et je crois que, s'il en savait quelque chose, l'espérance d'être aimé de vous et les traitements qu'il reçoit de moi, l'obligeraient bientôt à me quitter.' Félime's pessimistic interpretation is quite the opposite of Zaïde's. She protests that she would die if Alamir were to discover the truth, for it would remove

---

[11] Cf. Zaïde's fear of being heard and understood by Consalve, and Consalve's opposite reaction: 'quoiqu'il fît assez de bruit, elle parlait avec tant d'attention qu'elle ne l'entendit point. Lorsqu'il fut devant elle, elle parut embarrassée comme une personne qui venait de parler haut, qui craignait qu'on n'eût entendu ce qu'elle avait dit et qui avait oublié que Consalve ne pouvait l'entendre [. . .] Consalve [. . .] se jeta tout d'un coup à ses genoux et lui parla de son amour d'une manière si passionnée qu'il n'était pas nécessaire d'entendre ses paroles pour savoir ce qu'elles voulaient dire' (93).

her last vestige of hope—she prefers to cling to the illusion that he might love her if only he knew her feelings, rather than face probable rejection (174). Moreover, she believes that by adhering to the rules of *bienséance* and hiding her love, she will be protected from the worst excesses of suffering.

It is significant that Félime should associate confessing her love to Alamir with dying. When Zaïde suggests that Alamir should be told of her feelings for him, Félime retorts: 'Ah! Zaïde, ne m'ôtez pas la seule chose qui m'empêche de mourir de douleur; je ne survivrais pas à celle que j'aurais si Alamir avait appris mes sentiments' (174). After this conversation with Zaïde, she does in fact break her vow of silence three times, each time moving closer to her death. Her first and inadvertent breach of *bienséant* reticence comes when she realizes that Alamir has overheard her telling Zaïde of her feelings. She reacts with horror, knowing that speech cannot be taken back once uttered, and her wish to suppress the words she has just spoken takes the form of a wish for self-extinction: 'Les forces me manquèrent; je perdis la parole; je souhaitai la mort' (200). From her perspective, self-expression and self-preservation are incompatible. Her second confession comes when she reluctantly agrees to tell her story to Don Olmond because she believes that doing so will save Alamir's life, and she describes the breaking of her silence as 'la chose du monde que j'aurais le moins cru pouvoir obtenir de moi-même' (163). Once she has told her story her health deteriorates rapidly (226), and on her third confession, when she finally breaks down at Alamir's deathbed and tells him of her love, she dies (230).

In the character of Félime, Madame de Lafayette exemplifies the fears and dangers not only of female self-revelation but of female narration itself. It is ironic that the only one of the novel's stories to be narrated in a female voice (the 'Histoire de Zaïde et de Félime') should be told by the character who is most conscious of the risks of such a procedure. Her caution is justified. When she reluctantly confides her story to Don Olmond, she prefaces it with the injunction, 'Gardez-moi un secret inviolable' (163). But as the reader has come to expect from Madame de Lafayette's loquacious male characters, Don Olmond immediately breaches the confidence and repeats all that he has learned: 'Don Olmond [. . .] fit un récit exact de tout ce qu'il avait su par Félime' (204). By the time we reach the second half of her story (the 'Suite de l'histoire de Félime et de Zaïde'), Félime's voice has been suppressed: Don Olmond takes over her tale and narrates it himself. Her secrets have been appropriated and made public against her will, and Alamir's life—the condition on which she breached her silence—is not saved. Her experience can be read as yet another of Madame de Lafayette's bitter examples of the risks inherent in a woman's exposing herself through language.[12]

But it is through the portrayal of Zaïde herself that these issues find their sharpest focus. Enigmatic and largely silent or absent, she is most frequently presented to us through others: Consalve gives us his (false) view of her, and even when that is finally corrected by the 'Histoire de Zaïde et de Félime', it is not the voice of Zaïde herself that tells her story but those of Félime, Don Olmond and, finally, her father. By offering so little textual presence to her eponymous heroine, Madame de Lafayette paradoxically draws special attention to her. This paradox is central to the novel: the problematization of her absence and silence lets us see beyond the illusory fictional world to a real problem which Madame de Lafayette first explored in her *Portrait de Madame de Sévigné*. If we do not accept Zaïde's erasure (and the title urges us not to), we may read her silences and misunderstood speech as another example of Madame de Lafayette working to give metaphorical expression to the unsayable. Together with the suppressed voice and desire of Félime, these silences and misunderstandings not only represent the impossibility of real communication between men and women, but dramatize Madame de Lafayette's own ambiguous voice that simultaneously speaks and suppresses itself. Foreshadowing the dilemmas facing the Princesse de Clèves, they are, perhaps, also echoes of the author's own conflicting attitudes towards expressing herself in writing.

---

[12] In this case, the example is not completely unambiguous. Félime's silence does preserve her dignity to a certain extent, but it cannot alleviate her suffering.

CHAPTER 6

❖

La Princesse de Clèves

The withholding of Madame de Lafayette's name from the title-page of her masterpiece, *La Princesse de Clèves*, was not, as we have seen, entirely innocent. The novel's fame had spread rapidly through private salon readings before publication,[1] and when the work did finally appear, it was prefaced by a note which purported to explain why the author wished to remain anonymous:

Quelque approbation qu'ai[t] eu[e] cette Histoire dans les lectures qu'on en a faites, l'auteur n'a pu se résoudre à se déclarer; il a craint que son nom ne diminuât le succès de son livre. Il sait par expérience que l'on condamne quelquefois les ouvrages sur la médiocre opinion qu'on a de l'auteur et il sait aussi que la réputation de l'auteur donne souvent du prix aux ouvrages. Il demeure donc dans l'obscurité où il est, pour laisser les jugements plus libres et plus équitables, et il se montrera néanmoins si cette Histoire est aussi agréable au public que je l'espère. (239)

It has been argued that Madame de Lafayette, in withholding her signature from *La Princesse de Clèves*, was attempting to focus the reader's attention on the text rather than on its author.[2] But this note to the reader has quite the opposite effect, directing our attention to the mysterious author and holding out the tantalizing possibility that the enigma of his identity (for again, the anonymous disguise is a male one) may soon be revealed. Operating in the same way as the disclaimer that prefaces *La Princesse de Montpensier*, the note draws attention to what it pretends to silence. It therefore serves as a particularly fitting introduction to *La Princesse de Clèves*, where Madame de Lafayette explores with greater subtlety than ever before the familiar

---

[1] Cf. J.-B. de Valincour, *Lettres à Madame la Marquise *** sur le sujet de 'La Princesse de Clèves'* (Paris: Mabre-Cramoisy, 1678), Première lettre, 4: 'on l'avoit annoncé longtemps avant sa naissance; [. . .] l'on peut dire, qu'il est peu de livres, qui ayent apres l'impression, une approbation aussi générale, que l'a eûë celui-ci, avant mesme que d'avoir esté veu du public.'

[2] DeJean, 'Lafayette's Ellipses', 887.

theme of the power-play that lies behind the tensions between silence and speech.

It was that very aspect of the novel which elicited most response from its first readers. The remarkable reputation which the book had achieved before being published was vigorously exploited by Donneau de Visé in his attempts to relaunch his journal, *Le Mercure galant*. In an unprecedented publicity campaign, readers of *Le Mercure galant* were invited to engage in a debate about whether the Princess should have told her husband of her love for another man, or remained silent. Soon the novel had stirred up a spirited controversy,[3] and it has remained a focus of critical attention ever since, inspiring a vast range of commentary over the past three hundred years.[4] That *La Princesse de Clèves* should continue to intrigue is evidence of its fundamental ambiguity. It defies reductive interpretations because its positions are never fully stated and so can never be pinned down. Full of those apparent contradictions and tensions which we have seen in Madame de Lafayette's earlier works, it reflects a fundamental unease in the face of dissolving or conflicting values.

Nowhere are those tensions portrayed more clearly than in the novel's treatment of marriage. Marriage features in all its forms—anticipated, arranged, celebrated, betrayed and broken—and the text contains no fewer than 106 references to forty-one different marriages.[5] Through them, Madame de Lafayette explores many of the ideas which formed part of a long and continuing contemporary debate about the institution of marriage.[6] Questions such as whether marriage should be seen as a holy sacrament or as a secular or political alliance; whether the will of the marriage partners should outweigh the wishes of their parents; the place of passion in marriage; the relative authority of Church and State—all are examined and

[3] See *Le Mercure galant* (Apr., July and Oct. 1678—*Extraordinaire*—and Mar., May and Oct. 1678—*Ordinaire*); also Valincour, *Lettres à Madame la Marquise* ***; and the *Conversations sur la critique de 'La Princesse de Clèves'* (Paris: Barbin, 1679), believed to be the work of the Abbé de Charnes.

[4] Laugaa, *Lectures de Madame de Lafayette*, gives a useful selection of criticism of the novel since its publication.

[5] The calculation is Pierre Malandain's. See his 'Ecriture de l'histoire dans *La Princesse de Clèves*', *Littérature* 36 (Dec. 1979), 19–36 (esp. 26 n. 15).

[6] See Christian Biet, 'Droit et fiction: la représentation du mariage dans *La Princesse de Clèves*', in *Mme de La Fayette, La Princesse de Montpensier, La Princesse de Clèves*, ed. Roger Duchêne and Pierre Ronzeaud, *Littératures Classiques* (Supplément 1990) (Paris: 1989), 33–54.

discussed, but no solution to these conflicts is proposed. Madame de Lafayette introduces the central issues in the first pages of the novel. Henri II's marriage to Catherine de Médicis and his twenty-year-long passion for his mistress firmly establishes a distinction between love and marriage;[7] the reference in the novel's second paragraph to Madame de Valentinois's grand-daughter, Mademoiselle de la Marck, 'qui était alors à marier', raises the question of how a spouse is chosen; and the first two marriages mentioned in the description of the splendour of Henri II's court evoke the potential risks and suffering involved. The veiled allusion to the subsequent death of Madame Elisabeth de France—widely believed to have been poisoned by her husband, the King of Spain—is immediately followed by a reference to the ill-fated Mary Queen of Scots. As the description of the court continues, Madame de Lafayette introduces more variations on the marriage question. The soaring status of the Guise brothers is brought about by their niece's marriage to the Dauphin;[8] the new matrimonial powers of the monarch are demonstrated by the King's intervention, against the wishes of the Church, in setting aside the Connétable's eldest son's clandestine marriage to a maid of honour, so that he can marry Diane de France in accordance with his father's orders. The increasing powers of paternal authority are repeatedly evoked throughout this introductory section. The Cardinal de Lorraine heads a family where all marriages conform to the family interest, and where the Chevalier de Guise, as a younger son, obediently forgoes his hopes of marrying Mlle de Chartres and seeks military glory instead. Even the disobedient sons of the Connétable, who initially follow their private passions instead of dynastic interests, reluctantly agree to enter into marriages which will consolidate their father's power.

At this early stage in the novel, as at the beginning of many of Madame de Lafayette's writings, the emphasis appears to be on authority and respect for order. That the established order may be

[7] Other royal instances of the dangers of combining passion and marriage include the Dauphine's account of how Henri II almost divorced the Queen in order to marry the Dauphine's mother, whom he loved, and the disorder unleashed by Henry VIII when he allowed passion to take priority over political expediency in his marriages.

[8] 'MM. de Guise, dont elle était nièce, avaient beaucoup augmenté leur crédit et leur considération par son mariage; leur ambition les faisait aspirer à s'égaler aux princes du sang et à partager le pouvoir du connétable de Montmorency' (244).

transient is barely hinted at. When we read in the opening sentence that 'La magnificence et la galanterie n'ont jamais paru en France avec tant d'éclat que dans les dernières années du règne de Henri second' (241), we are made aware that a comparison is being drawn with the authorial present, and that the court has diminished in splendour since the time of Henri II. But that initial hint is immediately suppressed. In seeming contradiction to the transience implicit in the opening words, the first page instead goes on to emphasize the unchanging nature of this court, dominated for more than twenty years by the King's undiminished passion for the Duchesse de Valentinois, and characterized by a daily ritual of ballets, hunts, tilting at the ring and tennis matches, which continues without interruption.

But these games and pastimes are not merely innocent pleasures. Instead, they may be seen as a metaphor for court society. Just as Louis XIV's passion for the game of 'portiques' (as described in the *Mémoires de la cour de France*) reflects the importance of luck rather than good management in the course of the war, here the incessant manœuvres of rivalry, feint and display which these entertainments involve are analogous to the everyday movements of the courtiers. As courtiers and as players the characters of the novel are constrained by codes of conduct which they try to turn to their own advantage in order to win. The games and dances offer a ludic representation of life at court, emphasizing the strict rules that govern acceptable behaviour. But they also suggest the possibility that these rules may be transgressed. The jousting and tourneying allow the courtiers to play out a challenge to the established hierarchy in the form of mock battles whose threat to authority is hidden by the ritual of the game. And the structure of the court ball permits—indeed, compels—the Princess to come into close physical contact with Nemours to a degree that court etiquette would forbid in any other circumstance, while the delicate manœuvres of the dance, with constantly changing partners, are an authorized reflection of the intrigues in which the men and women of the court are secretly engaged.[9]

These courtly diversions reach their peak with the tournament ordered by the King to celebrate three simultaneous and triumphant achievements: the signing of the peace treaty with Spain, the marriage of the King's daughter Elisabeth to the King of Spain, and the

---

[9] For a discussion of the ball as 'une transgression réglée de la vie', see Malandain, 'Ecriture de l'histoire dans *La Princesse de Clèves*', 19–36 (esp. 26).

marriage of the King's sister to the Duc de Savoie. Each of these three events can be seen as an apparent confirmation of the prevailing code: the Franco-Spanish treaty seems to proclaim a period of order with peace ensured and the King's supremacy unchallenged both at home and abroad, while the two marriages emphasize the dynastic importance of matrimonial alliances by cementing the power of the monarchy. Moreover, Elisabeth's marriage demonstrates the force of paternal authority: she yields to her father's will in spite of the repugnance she feels for the King of Spain, and her agreement to submit to this marriage is a clear example of the subordination of personal desire to the demands and duties of dynastic, political and paternal interests. Holding the tournament is a means of reinforcing and transmitting these values by carrying the effects of the celebration far beyond the narrow confines of the court: 'Il [le roi] résolut de faire un tournoi, où les étrangers seraient reçus, et dont le peuple pourrait être spectateur' (304). The tournament's full programme is announced throughout the kingdom, together with the precise rules which the contestants must follow. Madame de Lafayette lays particular emphasis on this by reproducing the document in a lengthy and detailed paragraph whose extreme formality of language and instructions echoes the socially controlling intention of the celebratory ritual.

But in this novel of suspect values, this apparent stability and control soon prove to be illusory. The public rules of court behaviour which stress monogamy, obedience, loyalty and secrecy are manipulated or openly flouted by protagonists engaged in a struggle for power. The careful planning of the tournament and its rules of combat prove insufficient to contain and control events. In an incident which prefigures their loss of mastery, Nemours and the King, both excellent horsemen, momentarily lose control of their mounts during the preparations for the tournament, and Nemours is unseated and injured; at the tournament itself the King is killed. Both of these accidents have far-reaching consequences which disrupt the status quo, reversing the established hierarchy and heralding disorder. Nemours's fall causes the Princess to reveal her feelings both to him and to the Duc de Guise; her realization that 'elle n'était plus maîtresse de cacher ses sentiments' (307) precipitates her confession and the novel's dénouement. And the King's death brings about a complete transformation of the hierarchy of power at court as new alliances are formed and once powerful figures are banished. In other words, both the rules of play carefully delineated for the tournament and the rules of courtly conduct itself are disrupted. The court's pastimes thus illustrate tensions between strict codes of conduct and the transgression of those norms, between an established hierarchy of power and the undermining of its values.

As the novel unfolds, these currents of tension—already familiar from Madame de Lafayette's other works—become increasingly evident. They focus especially on the dilemma facing the Princesse de Clèves, but her particular situation is refracted through the forty other marriages presented in the novel. Her mother, Madame de Chartres, offers a formulation of the 'ideal' marriage.[10] Her advice to her daughter emphasizes the importance of fidelity in women and the misery that results from amorous intrigues; she tells her that an 'honnête femme' can find marital happiness only if she loves and is loved by her husband. Madame de Chartres's advice echoes the conventional definition of the highly regarded 'honnête femme' as a woman who is pious, subservient, reticent and faithful to her husband.[11] Critics have rightly stressed the importance of Madame de Chartres's influence. They point out that she and her daughter arrive as newcomers at a court which is full of corruption and intrigue, and that the Princess's dilemma stems from her desire to remain true to the virtuous example instilled by her mother, in circumstances where such behaviour is exceptional.

However, the counsel, warnings and examples which Madame de Chartres sets out for her daughter are far from unambiguous, for there are significant discrepancies between Madame de Chartres's advice and her action. For all her talk of the importance of loving and being loved by one's husband, she does not take this factor into consideration at all during her skilled and complex negotiations to secure a suitable mate for her daughter. Instead, her selection is motivated by ambition and by spite at the Duc de Nevers's rebuff. When her

---

[10] Madame de Chartres herself follows in a tradition of mothers depicted in novels by women at that time, and it has been argued that she can be seen as a mouthpiece for a particularly male-dominant class whose social and moral values she attempts to uphold. See A. Kibedi Varga, 'Romans d'amour, romans de femmes, à l'époque classique', *Revue des sciences humaines* 168 (1977), 517–24 (esp. 523). Other examples cited by Varga are *La Comtesse de Mortanes* by Madame Bédacier, and *Eléonore d'Yvrée* by Mlle Bernard.

[11] See Maclean, 123 and 152. Note that the definition of 'honnêteté' as applied to men ('accompli en toute sorte de perfections et de vertus') made no reference to marital fidelity.

scheme to marry Mlle de Chartres to the Prince Dauphin fails, the description of the bitterness of the mother's injured pride and dashed hopes for social advancement and revenge, and the omission of any reference to the daughter's feelings, begin to undermine our confidence in Madame de Chartres's advice: 'L'on peut juger ce que sentit Mme de Chartres par la rupture d'une chose qu'elle avait tant désirée, dont le mauvais succès donnait un si grand avantage à ses ennemis et faisait un si grand tort à sa fille' (255). It is clear, then, that Madame de Chartres is driven by a desire for power rather than by her professed concern that her daughter should be able to love her marriage partner.

Similarly, her admonition to Mlle de Chartres to confide in her at all times can be seen less as a means of protecting her daughter than as a way of ensuring continued authority over her.[12] In Madame de Chartres's behaviour we can see the workings of a power strategy which is extremely widespread at court, and which Madame de Lafayette described in detail in her *Histoire de Madame*. By eliciting confidences, encouraging a proliferation of 'secret' discourse and bringing into the open that which is personal and private, Madame de Chartres attempts to contain and control her daughter's behaviour.

Moreover, although Madame de Chartres is described as a woman 'dont le bien, la vertu et le mérite étaient extraordinaires' (247), one little-noted reference raises doubts as to whether her 'virtue' is really so unlike that of the other women at court. Madame de Chartres makes a mysterious reference to a beautiful woman who secretly loves and is loved by the Duc d'Orléans, and who on the same day learns that both the Duke and her husband have died. She is thus able to conceal her grief at her lover's death as she mourns her husband. Madame de Chartres does not name this woman, who, she says, has since lived such a virtuous and prudent life and has hidden her affair so completely that she deserves to keep her good reputation (267–8). How, one wonders, can Madame de Chartres know about so secret

---

[12] Marianne Hirsch has argued that while Madame de Chartres purports to offer her daughter the key to independence, self-determination and autonomy by warning her about the dangers of men, she in effect enslaves her in another form of dependence. As the Princess progressively internalizes her mother's advice, Hirsch sees her following a 'typically female form of development through self-denial' which is also 'a form of extinction, a death-warrant passed on to the daughter by her mother'. See 'A Mother's Discourse: Interpretation and Repetition in *La Princesse de Clèves*', *Yale French Studies* 62 (1981), 67–87.

a passion? The most natural explanation is that the woman in question is none other than Madame de Chartres herself—she is, after all, a beautiful widow who retired from court on the death of her husband; and she shows no such reticence about conveying the identity of other women she holds up to her daughter as warnings. This intriguing detail, generally overlooked by critics, might be taken simply as an explanation for Madame de Chartres's wish to ensure that her daughter does not make the same mistake. But if it is seen in the context of the framework of rules and models that structure the novel, a further interpretation is possible: this suppressed example offers the Princess an alternative to her mother's professed advice. Madame de Chartres (if it was indeed she) was one of the most beautiful women at court, who, although married, loved and was loved by a handsome, ambitious and daring Prince; but she kept her feelings so secret 'qu'elle a mérité que l'on conserve sa réputation'. The lesson implicit here would seem to be that secrecy and discretion are more important for one's reputation than actual behaviour—a lesson that runs counter to the rest of Madame de Chartres's teaching. Despite the uncompromising clarity of her advice, Madame de Chartres, like other important female characters in Madame de Lafayette's fiction, in fact reflects a tension between different possible modes of behaviour. As we shall see later, this unspoken and triumphant confession, where guilt *becomes* virtue and where 'sagesse' and 'réputation' are won by keeping silent, may be the most important lesson that the Princesse de Clèves learns from her mother.

But Madame de Chartres is not the Princess's only model. In the novel's opening pages Madame de Lafayette introduces two other important figures of female authority whose influence is highly significant: Diane de Poitiers, the Duchesse de Valentinois, and Catherine de Médicis, the Queen. These two women, readily recognized by the reader as real historical figures and who therefore carry additional exemplarity, seem at first to embody opposite poles of female behaviour. Madame de Valentinois is the first woman to be mentioned, and her presence, either in person or in symbolic form, pervades the court: 'les couleurs et les chiffres de Mme de Valentinois paraissaient partout, et elle paraissait elle-même' (241). Like her 'couleurs' and 'chiffres' at court, her moral presence suffuses the novel even when she herself is absent. More important, she is a living rebuttal of Madame de Chartres's advice to her daughter. She openly flouts the accepted behaviour of an 'honnête femme'. Like the

Marquise de Noirmoutier in *La Princesse de Montpensier*, who 'prenait autant de soin de faire éclater ses galanteries que les autres en prennent de les cacher' (33), Madame de Valentinois makes no secret of her many lovers. While Madame de Chartres tries to imbue her daughter with the conventions of female *honnêteté* as a means of avoiding being betrayed by men, the Duchess, like the Marquise de Noirmoutier, presents a contrary model by inspiring undying passion through very different conduct. As Madame de Chartres is forced to concede, 'Il est vrai [. . .] que ce n'est ni le mérite, ni la fidélité de Mme de Valentinois qui a fait naître la passion du roi, ni qui l'a conservée' (264). Most important of all, her powers are not limited to the royal bedroom, for Madame de Valentinois is the most powerful person in the kingdom, more powerful even than the King himself: 'elle le gouvernait avec un empire si absolu que l'on peut dire qu'elle était maîtresse de sa personne et de l'Etat' (244).[13]

But the opening paragraphs of the novel indicate that the Duchesse de Valentinois's absolute authority is already compromised; the picture of court life which will follow is based on a precarious balance of power. The Duchesse de Valentinois may be said to have complete dominion over both King and State, but for her very presence at court she is dependent on the Queen, Catherine de Médicis: 'La présence de la reine autorisait la sienne' (241). The Queen, however, needs the Duchess if she is to remain close to the King: 'la politique l'obligeait d'approcher cette duchesse de sa personne, afin d'en approcher aussi le roi' (242). The two women are presented as mutually dependent opposites. The Duchesse de Valentinois has been loved by two kings, and the strength of Henri II's feelings for her have remained undiminished for more than twenty years. The Queen, on the other hand, is twice betrayed by men—first by her husband the King, and then by the Vidame de Chartres. The Duchesse de Valentinois's strength derives from the passion she inspires; the Queen's power comes from her constitutional position.

These two women represent the most outstanding examples of a complex network of female intrigue at court, similar in many respects to the web of strategic manœuvres described in the *Histoire de Madame*. As in the *Histoire*, the love affairs and 'galanteries' on which the plot focuses must be seen in terms of bids for power and control:

---

[13] Cf. *Histoire de Madame*, 26, where Mlle de Mancini is described as 'la maîtresse d'un prince que nous avons vu depuis maître de sa maîtresse et de son amour'.

Il y avait tant d'intérêts et tant de cabales différentes, et les dames y avaient tant de part que l'amour était toujours mêlé aux affaires et les affaires à l'amour. Personne n'était tranquille, ni indifférent; on songeait à s'élever, à plaire, à servir ou à nuire; on ne connaissait ni l'ennui, ni l'oisiveté, et on était toujours occupé des plaisirs ou des intrigues. Les dames avaient des attachements particuliers pour la reine, pour la reine dauphine, pour la reine de Navarre, pour Madame, sœur du roi, ou pour la duchesse de Valentinois. (252)

As the juxtaposition of 'plaisirs' and 'intrigues' here suggests, women's drive for influence is perceived as a strong and enjoyable one. To become a 'maîtresse' is to win mastery as well as love. Yet at the same time Madame de Lafayette shows that, when all is said and done, this female power is precarious and predicated on men. Even Madame de Valentinois, 'maîtresse [. . .] de l'Etat', loses all importance once the King has died, and the Queen merely exchanges one master for another, for the Cardinal de Lorraine makes himself 'maître absolu de [son] esprit' after her husband's death (358). The heroine is thus presented with a conflicting range of models of behaviour—none fully satisfactory—in a court which projects the superficial appearance of stability and strict etiquette, but where in reality everyone is engaged in a subtle play for power in a context of dissolving values.

Set against these dubious and inconsistent examples, the Princess herself initially lacks definition. When she makes her first appearance in the novel she is presented conventionally through her social position as her family background, status, inheritance and appearance are enumerated. Yet, as in *La Comtesse de Tende* and *La Princesse de Montpensier*, that conventional introduction will prove to be inadequate. She is introduced a second time through the eyes of M. de Clèves, whose reaction on first seeing her is not unlike that of Consalve on seeing Zaïde: he is amazed and puzzled. She, like Zaïde, is an enigma to men. At the Italian jeweller's where Clèves first encounters her, she seems to fit into none of the expected categories. The jeweller does not know who she is, and mistakenly calls her 'Madame'. M. de Clèves cannot understand where she can have come from; he cannot tell whether or not she is married; he is surprised that someone of her beauty should be embarrassed by his obvious admiration, and even more amazed to discover that no one knows who she is. In contrast to her initial introduction, this second presentation shows her as an anonymous stranger, as the embodiment of the male myth of woman as enigma. As Clèves says on a later occasion, 'les femmes sont incompréhensibles' (280). His reaction to his first encounter with Mlle de Chartres is to talk about his experience, endlessly: 'il ne pouvait parler d'autre chose. Il conta tout haut son aventure, et ne pouvait se lasser de donner des louanges à cette personne qu'il avait vue, qu'il ne connaissait point' (250). Like Consalve, his instinct is to turn his experiences, real or imaginary, into language, but the linguistic vision he conjures up cannot replicate the object of his desire, and Madame, to whom he describes her, denies the very existence of his idol: 'Madame lui dit qu'il n'y avait point de personne comme celle qu'il dépeignait et que, s'il y en avait quelqu'une, elle serait connue de tout le monde' (250). So that second introduction, too, is shown to be inadequate; like others of Madame de Lafayette's heroines, the Princess is resistant to both these means of categorizing her (by family and inheritance, and by an uncomprehending male admirer). The fact that Mlle de Chartres visits the jeweller unaccompanied by her mother, an act of independence that misleads both the Italian and Clèves into doubting that she can be an unmarried woman, is the first tiny hint that the heroine may possess certain unconventional qualities. As Madame de Chartres comments, 'si vous jugez sur les apparences en ce lieu-ci [. . .] vous serez souvent trompée: ce qui paraît n'est presque jamais la vérité' (265)—an observation which is as true for the way in which we read Madame de Lafayette's narrative as it is for the intrigues at court.

The suggestion that the Princess may not be the conventionally passive cipher she first appears gains force as Madame de Lafayette shows her gradually and tentatively exploring alternatives to the examples offered by women such as Madame de Chartres, the Queen and Madame de Valentinois and moving slowly towards self-determination. After being introduced, like Zaïde, as a mysterious and passive object, the Princess will gradually develop her own discreet strategies to protect herself from the fates of the women around her. As the novel progresses, it becomes clear that in her dealings with both Clèves and Nemours the Princess is playing out her own variation of the games of love and power that surround her at court. Initially unreflecting, she follows scrupulously the code of behaviour deemed most proper for a woman, obeying the rules of reticence, passivity, fidelity, modesty and filial piety. Her reputation is secure, and she is regarded by all as a model of charm, obedience and reserve.

Yet it is through her own particular use of these conventional traits that she comes to forge her own inner strength and independence until, at the end, she can be defined as an 'inimitable' individual.

Some recent critics have argued that *La Princesse de Clèves* shows Madame de Lafayette using this aspect of the work to make a strongly feminist statement. Roger Gaillard's view is that 'le long chemin lumineux et terrible de Madame de Clèves est celui de la prise d'individualité par la prise de parole' and that Madame de Lafayette has portrayed, through the Princess, one woman's struggle to assert her own individuality and desires in the face of a stifling male pressure to conform.[14] Her confession, transgressing conventional codes of female behaviour, is seen by Gaillard as her first step towards breaking with the world of male values, for once she has spoken out, he argues, her words have far-reaching consequences; not only has she proved herself to be different, but she has plunged her husband into an unstable world where nothing follows the norm. Faced with the Princess's claim that her confession is a mark of her faithfulness, Clèves is unable to accept it and instead becomes fatally convinced of the very opposite—her love for, and seduction by, Nemours. 'En fin de compte, l'aveu a pris le visage d'un meurtrier symbolique.'[15] Once Clèves has died, argues Gaillard, the will and energy of the Princess increase, while Nemours becomes a pale shadow of his former character. Her farewell to him is the expression of her ultimate achievement—her detachment from her former state, and the beginning of her assertion of her true self. 'Le roman de Madame de Lafayette est celui d'une femme qui pose sa force entre le moi et ses objets, en habitant petit à petit sa parole', concludes Gaillard.[16]

Joan DeJean, too, sees the 'aveu' as crucial because it marks the heroine's attempt to take control: she argues that in her account of the confession the author 'transforms the revelation of forbidden love from a scene of female weakness to a conquest of language (*prise de parole*) that is at the same time an initiation into writing, the act by which the Princess first lays title to her own story.'[17] For DeJean, the novel is an account of 'the heroine's gradual determination to supervise the plot of her life'.

But it is difficult to reconcile Madame de Lafayette's text with such

---

[14] Roger Gaillard, *Approche de . . . la Princesse de Clèves* (Dijon: Editions de l'Aleï, 1983), 21.
[15] Ibid. 22. [16] Ibid. 25. [17] DeJean, 'Lafayette's Ellipses', 897.

an unambiguous message. In the midst of the court's all-pervasive talk of 'galanteries' and clandestine amours, the Princess is remarkable for her silence. She is frequently urged by others to talk, and her reactions are generally evasive. The passage where Clèves first tells her of his love is typical: when he declares his passion, pressing her to say what are her true feelings for him, her reply has 'un certain air de douceur qui suffisait pour donner de l'espérance à un homme aussi éperdument amoureux que l'était ce prince; de sorte qu'il se flatta d'une partie de ce qu'il souhaitait' (257). Her response is characteristically elusive, and it is Clèves himself who gives it meaning. Despite feminist claims that she moves towards self-definition through the gradual discovery of her own voice, the text does not allow such an unproblematic interpretation. It is true that the Princess does progress beyond the initial state of paralysis caused by her conflicting senses of duty, a state which is seen most clearly in the description of her reaction to Nemours's indirect declarations of love: 'Il lui semblait qu'elle devait y répondre et ne les pas souffrir. Il lui semblait aussi qu'elle ne devait pas les entendre, ni témoigner qu'elle les prît pour elle. Elle croyait devoir parler et croyait ne devoir rien dire [. . .] Elle demeurait donc sans répondre' (294). But what follows that silence of uncertainty can hardly be called a *prise de parole*.

   The closest the Princess comes to an assertive use of language is at the mid-point of the novel, when, alone with Nemours, she attempts to recreate the lost letter from Madame de Thémines. The original letter, with its insistence on personal expression ('je' appears fifty-eight times in these two pages), its confident analysis of motives and strategies, its recognition and acceptance of passion and all the suffering, jealousy and risk that it entails, its overt manœuvring for sexual power, its delight in revenge and in 'le plaisir de dissimuler' and, above all, its demonstration of the writer's self-awareness and self-assertion, stands in marked contrast to the Princess's own reticence. Little wonder that 'Mme de Clèves lut cette lettre et la relut plusieurs fois, sans savoir néanmoins ce qu'elle avait lu' (310). Yet detail by detail, it expresses her own dilemma—her horror of being considered 'légère', her feigning of illness to conceal emotions, her repeated making and breaking of resolutions, and her distress at the thought of betrayal. Moreover, it proposes a solution: the successful device of feigning rejection in order to secure and sustain the lover's passion. The letter's conclusion, however, casts this success aside: having triumphed over her rival and ensured the Vidame's love, Madame de

Thémines vows never to see him again. So when Madame de Clèves sits down with Nemours to copy the letter—or, rather, to reconstruct it, for the original is no longer available—she is in effect writing her own story, already complete with the ending in which the ensnared lover is finally vanquished. Constantly torn between the desire to speak and the fear of speaking, the Princess, for once, is able to proclaim her submerged will through this re-creative act, and we are told that in doing so she experiences the purest sense of joy and freedom she has ever had. But she cannot sustain this surge of expression. Her text is a poor imitation of Madame de Thémines's forceful original, and although from now on her life will follow the course she has inscribed, she never again experiences the joy of those moments, and retreats into silence.

But that very silence comes to be seen as a sign of strength rather than weakness. As the Princess herself says, 'j'ai de la force pour taire ce que je crois ne pas devoir dire' (335). What has come to be known as the 'confession scene' is perhaps the most striking example of her forceful use of omissions, circumlocutions and silences. Far from being an outright 'confession', let alone a *prise de parole*, the scene unfolds with a series of denials and suppressions by the Princess. 'Je n'ai rien de fâcheux dans l'esprit', is her evasive reply to her husband's initial suspicion; when he presses her further, she remains reticent: 'Il la pressa longtemps de les lui apprendre sans pouvoir l'y obliger; et, après qu'elle se fut défendue d'une manière qui augmentait toujours la curiosité de son mari, elle demeura dans un profond silence, les yeux baissés.' The core of her 'confession' is, paradoxically, a request not to be made to confess something which she cannot confess: 'Ne me contraignez point, lui dit-elle, à vous avouer une chose que je n'ai pas la force de vous avouer'. Her subsequent silence has, once again, to be given a meaning by her husband, who declares that it confirms his suspicions: 'Vous ne me dites rien, reprit-il, et c'est me dire que je ne me trompe pas.' When she does finally speak, it is to assure him that she has never shown any sign of weakness, and as the scene continues it becomes clear that her strategy of reticence has altered the balance of power: she now rises to her feet and it is M. de Clèves who begs *her* for forgiveness, praises her action, and asserts her moral triumph: 'Ayez pitié de moi vous-même, madame [. . .] et pardonnez si [. . .] je ne réponds pas, comme je dois, à un procédé comme le vôtre. Vous me paraissez plus digne d'estime et d'admiration que tout ce qu'il y a jamais eu de femmes au monde.' Far from marking the

Princess's conquest of language, this scene highlights her ability to withhold language to her own advantage and shows her strength in doing so. Nothing that her husband can say will make her give in, and her final reply is couched in a vocabulary of power and manipulation: 'Vous m'en presseriez inutilement, répliqua-t-elle; j'ai de la force pour taire ce que je crois ne pas devoir dire. L'aveu que je vous ai fait n'a pas été par faiblesse, et il faut plus de courage pour avouer cette vérité que pour entreprendre de la cacher.' At one and the same time she asserts the strength of her silence and claims credit for her courage in speaking out (although she has not done so).

This paradoxical and contradictory presentation of speech and silence continues to the very end of the novel. In the Princess's final conversation with Nemours, when they are 'en état de se parler pour la première fois', her frankness of speech astonishes, delights and shames her: 'elle ne se connaissait plus. Elle fut étonnée de ce qu'elle avait fait; elle s'en repentit; elle en eut de la joie: tous ses sentiments étaient pleins de trouble et de passion.' Yet the thrust of her argument is the same as that of Madame de Thémines's letter, which had also brought her intense pleasure but which ended with the rejection of the lover: in openly declaring her love, she is at the same time rejecting and silencing Nemours. 'Ne parlons point de cette aventure', she says; '[. . .] je vous conjure de m'écouter sans m'interrompre [. . .] Je vous conjure, par tout le pouvoir que j'ai sur vous, de ne chercher aucune occasion de me voir [. . .] La seule bienséance interdit tout commerce entre nous [. . .] Voici une conversation qui me fait honte' (389). But to these final, silencing words, her last in the novel, the Princess adds a paradoxical twist. She instructs Nemours to give an account of the 'shameful' conversation to the Vidame, whom she knows to be an inveterate gossip.

Madame de Lafayette offers no final resolution. Those critics who see the heroine's rejection of Nemours as evidence of her beginning to assert her true self,[18] or as an 'acte de victoire',[19] conveniently ignore the fact that she dies soon afterwards. In her final words the Princess describes the rare delight of self-expression, but also the shame and humiliation that may result; she shows the potential power of silence, but also the pain of self-denial; and she refuses any further discussion of her situation, yet makes sure that her story is told to the notoriously indiscreet Vidame.

[18] Gaillard, 25.   [19] A. Kibedi Varga, 524.

With a heroine who is torn between speaking and withholding speech, and who recognizes the dangers as well as the delights of open expression, *La Princesse de Clèves*, like Madame de Lafayette's other works, dramatizes the problems of finding a voice. It is therefore not surprising that Madame de Lafayette's familiar concern with anonymity and self-identification should frequently surface in this text. Just as she withholds her name from the title-page and further problematizes her own identity in the prefatory note, so in the body of the novel names and identities are repeatedly withheld or shown to be problematic. Much of the plot revolves around attempts to identify the authors of rumours or letters. Mlle de Chartres is wrongly called 'Madame' by the Italian jeweller and M. de Clèves has great difficulty in identifying her after that initial encounter. When they marry, he is surprised to find that her change of name does not alter her: 'M. de Clèves ne trouva pas que Mlle de Chartres eût changé de sentiment en changeant de nom' (260). Madame de Chartres refuses to disclose the name of the Duc d'Orléans's married lover to her daughter, and makes an explicit association between discretion, reputation and anonymity (267–8). Characters are repeatedly discussed in their presence by third parties who are unaware of their identity. Behind their strongly ambivalent reactions of distress coupled with pleasure on hearing their own thoughts and feelings discussed and analysed by others,[20] one may discern the displaced unease of the author, torn between the desire to acknowledge and to conceal her identity as writer.

Nemours provides an alternative example of these hesitations between self-revelation and self-concealment. He is described as being guilty of 'une imprudence assez ordinaire, qui est de parler en termes généraux de ses sentiments particuliers et de conter ses propres aventures sous des noms empruntés' (337–8), but unlike the Princess, who instinctively inclines towards reticence and silence, he wants and needs to tell the story. His perfunctory concealment of his identity therefore carries little conviction, and he tells the story of the confession to the Vidame in such a way as to make his own involvement in it obvious. That 'confidential' story circulates endlessly and

---

[20] e.g. the Dauphine's account of Nemours's anonymous beloved fills the Princess with 'reconnaissance et [. . .] tendresse' but also with 'poison' as she looks for the 'moyen de ne se pas reconnaître pour cette personne dont on ne savait point le nom' (291).

damagingly, passed on by the Vidame to Madame de Martigues, who tells the Reine-Dauphine, who tells both the Princess and Nemours. Meanwhile, the Princess's withholding of Nemours' name drives her husband to distraction: 'vous me cachez un nom qui me donne une curiosité avec laquelle je ne saurais vivre', he says.[21] The subsequent attempts by M. de Clèves and his wife to discover who is responsible for the circulating story of the confession is, of course, bound to fail, for they themselves are, unwittingly, its true authors; but the endeavour culminates in a curious movement which seeks to suppress the very story they are pursuing. Clèves tells the Princess that 'il s'agissait de faire voir que l'histoire que l'on avait contée était une fable où elle n'avait aucune part' (350). Once the story has been told, however, it cannot be silenced, and its destructive power ultimately destroys all three protagonists.

Recurring with such insistence in *La Princesse de Clèves*, these familiar questions of identity, authorship and anonymity echo Madame de Lafayette's own ambivalence about revealing herself through her writing. These self-reflexive patterns show her still developing and exploring the same issues that she had first raised, lightheartedly, in her *Portrait de Madame de Sévigné* almost twenty years earlier.

---

[21] Cf. the repetition of 'nommer' as Clèves later tries unsuccessfully to force the Princess to name Nemours: 'Comme il vit qu'elle ne lui nommait point M. de Nemours, il lui demanda, en tremblant, si c'était tout ce qu'elle avait vu, afin de lui donner lieu de nommer ce prince et de n'avoir pas la douleur qu'elle lui en fît une finesse. Comme elle ne l'avait point vu, elle ne le lui nomma point' (361).

CHAPTER 7

❖

Conclusion

It is clear that a tension between reticence and revelation runs through all Madame de Lafayette's writings, where female modesty and silence are often closely bound up with a concern for power and prestige, although rarely in a straightforward and unambiguous way. She seems particularly sensitive to the conflicting demands of convention and ambition, propriety and desire, and she constantly hints at impending disruption to the apparently stable social order. Crosscurrents of contradiction run beneath the deceptively limpid prose. Although much of her writing explores ways in which silence can be used as an instrument of power, it also demonstrates the potential benefits of free expression; although it shows the dangers of speech, it also conveys the pain of self-suppression. Madame de Lafayette comes to no clear resolution of these issues, leaving the tensions and contradictions to intrigue and provoke her readers as much today as they did when her works first circulated in the salons. The unresolved hesitations between finding a voice and keeping silent, between self-assertion and self-effacement, are as evident in the conduct and expression of her characters as they are in her own contradictory attitudes towards acknowledging her authorship. They recur both in her fictional works and in her histories, and do so with such extraordinary persistence that one may speculate about what unconscious drive kept forcing her creative imagination to reflect this tension.

It is significant that Madame de Lafayette's biographers differ greatly in their presentation of her character and behaviour, for these very discrepancies may help us to begin to understand the origins of the contradictions in her own work. Contemporary salon references to her as 'le brouillard' have contributed to one view of her as a quiet, dreamy, melancholy and ailing creature, 'baignant dans la paresse',[1] and as her reputation soared, she was repeatedly portrayed as possessing all the

---

[1] Cit. Alain Niderst, *'La Princesse de Clèves' de Madame de Lafayette* (Paris: Nizet, 1977), 17.

approved womanly virtues of reticence, modesty and *bienséance*, allied with exceptional sensitivity and literary genius.[2] But like her fiction, her life resists such simple categorization. Other biographers play down the quiet, passive side and instead stress her business acumen and her sound grasp of legal intricacies. They point to her skill in dealing with the complicated debts of the Lafayette family, her success in securing her sons' inheritance, and her responsibility for the running of the family estates, including the right to sell her own properties. They present her as an ambitious intriguer, and argue that it was largely as the result of her skilful machinations at court that the Chevalier de Lorraine, Monsieur's favourite, was sent into exile; and they also stress her key role in Piedmontese politics when she served as an official agent for Jeanne-Baptiste de Savoie, carrying diplomatic secrets and acting as intermediary between the courts of Savoy and France. Far from being a model of quiet female modesty, she is seen by these biographers as forceful and active. For Roger Duchêne, for example, 'Elle a joué dans la vie un rôle d'homme'.[3]

The contradictory nature of these views of her involvement in public affairs is echoed by the conflicting accounts of her private life. Married at the late age of 20 to a man eighteen years older than herself, Madame de Lafayette is painted by some biographers as a dedicated wife working tirelessly to further the family fortunes, whose presence in Paris was dictated by the need to supervise family legal affairs there while her husband saw to the day-to-day running of their provincial estates. Yet others see her as a distant spouse who could not bear to be separated from the literary and courtly circles of the capital, and was happy to abandon her husband to the provinces and move back to Paris. At least one critic has claimed that Madame de Lafayette was the lover of Madame de Sévigné,[4] while Roger Duchêne has combed contemporary documents to find evidence for his contention that her incongruous marriage to Lafayette was hastily arranged in order to hide the fact that she was already pregnant. In his

---

[2] See Joan DeJean, 'Sappho's Leap: Domesticating the Woman Writer', *L'Esprit créateur* 25 (Summer 1985), 14–21. According to DeJean, 'the myth of Lafayette, the woman writer whose greatness eradicated all prior models for women's fiction, was created by the French critical tradition to camouflage its own subversive work' (17).

[3] Duchêne, *Madame de Lafayette*, 492.

[4] Claudine Herrmann, 'Madame de Lafayette et ses héroïnes tristes', preface to *Histoire de Madame Henriette d'Angleterre, La Princesse de Montpensier, La Comtesse de Tende* (Paris: Editions des Femmes, 1979), 14–16.

view, 'on sent tout autour d'elle un relent de libertinage de mœurs et de pensée'.[5]

That such contradictory visions of Madame de Lafayette can be entertained is in part attributable to the fact that she began to write at a time when crucial changes were taking place in France. Born in 1634, she spent most of her youth under the regency of Anne of Austria, the last in the series of queen-regents who had exercised an almost uninterrupted influence over French policy since 1560. But when Louis XIV assumed personal rule in 1661 the structure of the higher echelons of French society began to modify accordingly, and it became clear that what has been described as 'the heroic age [. . .] well known for the prominence enjoyed by women' was at an end.[6] At the same time, Madame de Lafayette found herself in an ambiguous social position. She was born into the 'petite noblesse' (her father had been an army officer specializing in fortifications, who subsequently became tutor to a nephew of Richelieu; her mother was lady-in-waiting to Richelieu's niece, the Duchesse d'Aiguillon), and although she married into a more distinguished family from the old provincial nobility, her marriage also brought heavy debts. Her circumstances would not normally have qualified her for an eminent position in Parisian society. But having been brought up in the orbit of Richelieu's family and with the Duchesse d'Aiguillon as her godmother, she had privileged contacts with the court. The *Histoire de Madame* clearly reveals Madame de Lafayette's social ambition and her desire to display her status as an intimate of the royal family, and all her work displays an acute awareness of the complex and subtle rules of social advancement.

It is therefore quite possible that the curious tensions and ambiguities discernible in her writing stem from her sense of a need for self-constraint in order to protect her tenuous social position—her birth and lineage would not normally have entitled her to such distinction, and so she adopts a mode of scrupulous *bienséance* so as not to jeopardize her precarious status. By publishing anonymously, she avoids the

---

[5] *Madame de Lafayette*, 47 and 9–15.

[6] Maclean, p. vii. Cf. ibid. 265: 'During these queen-regencies, the sense of the glorious present, the heroic deeds of female warriors, and literary activity by women seem to have opened up new horizons [. . .] Louis XIV's majority and the depreciation of the "morale héroïque" herald the return of the traditional moral order, and with it an attachment to firm divisions and the rule of common sense. The days of baroque feminism were over.'

risk of being taken for 'un vrai auteur de profession'. Nevertheless, the contradictions of her own temperament and behaviour show through in her writing, leaving traces of independence and assertiveness behind the apparent modesty and reticence. Madame de Lafayette remains protected by her 'privilège d'Inconnu' while she explores the ambiguity of her status as a woman and a writer.

BIBLIOGRAPHY

❖

ARONSON, NICOLE, *Mademoiselle de Scudéry ou le voyage au pays de Tendre* (Paris: Fayard, 1986).
ASCOLI, GEORGES, 'Essai sur l'histoire des idées féministes en France, du XVIe siècle à la Révolution', *Revue de synthèse historique* 13 (1906), 25–57; 99–106; 161–84.
BAILLET, ADRIEN, *Auteurs déguisez sous des noms étrangers; empruntez, supposez, feints à plaisir, chiffrez, renversez, retournez, ou changez d'une langue en une autre* (Paris: Dezallier, 1690).
—— *Jugemens des sçavans sur les principaux ouvrages des auteurs*, 5 vols. (Paris: Dezallier, 1685–6).
BAZIN, JEAN DE, *Index de vocabulaire. 'La Princesse de Montpensier', 'La Comtesse de Tende'* (Paris: Nizet, 1970).
—— *Index du vocabulaire de 'La Princesse de Clèves'* (Paris: Nizet, 1967).
BEASLEY, FAITH E., *Revising Memory: Women's Fiction and Memoirs in Seventeenth-Century France* (New Brunswick/London: Rutgers University Press, 1990).
BEAUNIER, A., 'Madame de Lafayette et Madame', *Revue de Paris* 33 (1926), 73–100.
BIET, CHRISTIAN, 'Droit et fiction: la représentation du mariage dans *La Princesse de Clèves*', in *Mme de La Fayette, La Princesse de Montpensier, La Princesse de Clèves*, ed. Roger Duchêne and Pierre Ronzeaud, *Littératures Classiques* (Supplément 1990) (Paris: 1989), 33–54.
BOSSUET, JACQUES-BÉNIGNE, 'Oraison funèbre de Henriette-Anne d'Angleterre, duchesse d'Orléans', in *Oraisons funèbres, panégyriques*, ed. Abbé Velat and Yvonne Champailler (Paris: Gallimard Pléïade, 1961).
BRIGGS, ROBIN, *Early Modern France 1560–1715* (Oxford: Oxford University Press, 1977).
BUSSY-RABUTIN, ROGER DE, *Correspondance*, ed. L. Lalanne, 6 vols. (Paris: Charpentier, 1858).
CASTRES, M. L'ABBÉ S*** DE, *Les Trois Siècles de la littérature française*, 5th edn. (La Haye, 1781).

CHAMARD, H., and RUDLER, G., 'Les sources historiques de *La Princesse de Clèves*', *Revue du seizième siècle* 2 (1914), 92–131 and 289–321.

CHARNES, ABBÉ DE, *Conversations sur la critique de 'La Princesse de Clèves'* (Paris: Barbin, 1679).

CHOISY, ABBÉ DE, *Mémoires de l'Abbé de Choisy habillé en femme*, in *Mémoires pour servir à l'Histoire de Louis XIV*, ed. G. Montgrédien (Paris: Mercure de France, 1966).

COR, ⅞. A., 'Games of Love and War in *La Princesse de Clèves*', *Kentucky Review Quarterly* 28 (1981), 131–8.

CUÉNIN, MICHELINE, 'La terreur sans la pitié: *La Comtesse de Tende*', *Revue d'histoire littéraire de la France* 77 (May–Aug. 1977), 478–99.

DALLAS, DOROTHY FRANCES, *Le Roman français de 1660 à 1680* (Geneva: Sklatine Reprints, 1977) (first pub. Paris, 1932).

DAVIS, NATALIE ZEMON, 'Gender and Genre: Women as Historical Writers, 1400–1820', in *Beyond Their Sex: Learned Women of the European Past*, ed. Patricia Labalme (New York, 1980), 153–82.

DEJEAN, JOAN, '*La Princesse de Clèves*: the Poetics of Suppression', *Papers on French Seventeenth-Century Literature* 10 (1983), 79–97.

—— 'Lafayette's Ellipses: the Privileges of Anonymity', *PMLA* 99 (Oct. 1984), 884–902.

—— 'Sappho's Leap: Domesticating the Woman Writer', *L'Esprit créateur* 25 (Summer 1985), 14–21.

DELACOMPTÉE, JEAN-MICHEL, *La Princesse de Clèves: la mère et le courtisan* (Paris: Presses Universitaires de France, 1990).

DUBOIS, ELFRIEDA, ' "Votre Sexe n'est là que pour la dépendance": Women and Marriage in Seventeenth-Century France', *Newsletter of the Society for Seventeenth-Century French Studies* 4 (1982), 14–26.

DUCHÊNE, ROGER, *Madame de Lafayette, la romancière aux cent bras* (Paris: Fayard, 1988).

DULONG, CLAUDE, *La Vie quotidienne des femmes au grand siècle* (Paris: Hachette, 1984).

DURRY, MARIE-JEANNE, *Madame de Lafayette* (Paris: Mercure de France, 1962).

ELIAS, NORBERT, *The Court Society*, trans. E. Jephcott (Oxford: Blackwell, 1983).

FÉNELON, FRANÇOIS DE SALIGNAC DE LA MOTHE, *De l'éducation des filles* (1687), ed. C. Defodon (Paris: Hachette, 1881).

FRANCILLON, ROGER, *L'Œuvre romanesque de Madame de Lafayette* (Paris: Corti, 1973).

FUMAROLI, MARC, *La Diplomatie de l'esprit. De Montaigne à La Fontaine* (Paris: Hermann, 1994).
GAILLARD, ROGER, *Approche de . . . La Princesse de Clèves* (Dijon: Editions de l'Aleï, 1983).
Galerie des peintures ou recueil des portraits et éloges en vers et en prose, La (1659, 2nd edn. Paris: de Seroy, 1663).
GENETTE, GÉRARD, 'Vraisemblance et motivation', in *Figures II* (Paris: Seuil, 1969), 71–99.
GENUIST, P., 'Pour une interprétation féministe de *La Princesse de Clèves*', *Papers on French Seventeenty-Century Literature* 9 (1978), 135–49.
HAIG, STIRLING, *Madame de Lafayette* (New York: Twayne, 1970).
HERRMANN, CLAUDINE, 'Madame de Lafayette et ses héroïnes tristes', preface to *Histoire de Madame Henriette d'Angleterre, La Princesse de Montpensier, La Comtesse de Tende* (Paris: Editions des Femmes, 1979).
HIPP, MARIE-THÉRÈSE, *Mythes et réalités. Enquête sur le roman et les mémoires (1660–1700)* (Paris: Klincksieck, 1976).
HIRSCH, MARIANNE, 'A Mother's Discourse: Interpretation and Repetition in *La Princesse de Clèves*', *Yale French Studies* 62 (1981), 67–87.
KAMUFF, PEGGY, *Fictions of Feminine Desire. Disclosures of Héloïse* (Lincoln and London: University of Nebraska Press, 1982).
KOTIN, ARMINE, 'La Canne des Indes. Lafayette lectrice de Madame de Villedieu', *Dix-septième siècle* 31 (1979), 409–11.
KIBEDI VARGA, A., 'Romans d'amour, romans de femmes, à l'époque classique', *Revue des sciences humaines* 168 (1977), 517–24.
KREITER, JANINE ANSEAUME, 'Introduction', in Madame de Lafayette, *Zaïde. Histoire espagnole* (Paris: Nizet, 1982), 7–23.
—— *Le Problème du paraître dans l'œuvre de Madame de Lafayette* (Paris: Nizet, 1977).
KUIZENGA, DONNA, *Narrative Strategies in 'La Princesse de Clèves'* (Lexington: French Forum, 1976).
LAFAYETTE, MARIE MADELEINE, comtesse de, *Correspondance*, ed. A. Beaunier, 2 vols. (Paris: Gallimard, 1942).
—— *Histoire de Madame Henriette d'Angleterre suivie de Mémoires de la cour de France pour les années 1688 et 1689*, ed. Gilbert Sigaux (Paris: Mercure de France, 1965).
—— *Romans et nouvelles*, ed. E. Magne (Paris: Garnier, 1970).
LANFREDI, DINA, 'Madame de Lafayette e Henriette d'Angleterre:

L'Histoire de Madame, con documenti inediti trattati dall'archivo di stato di Firenze', *Archivo Storico Italiano* 116 (1958), 178–206; 511–43.

LAUGAA, MAURICE, *Lectures de Madame de Lafayette* (Paris: Colin, 1971).

LEINER, WOLFGANG (ed.), *Onze Etudes sur l'image de la femme dans la littérature française du XVIIe siècle* (Tübingen: Gunter Narr Verlag, 1978).

LEMOINE, JEAN, 'Madame de La Fayette et Louvois', *Revue de Paris*, 14e année, no. 17 (1 Sept. 1907), 65–86.

LEVER, MAURICE, 'Romans en quête d'auteurs au XVIIe siècle', *Revue d'histoire littéraire de la France* 73 (1973), 7–21.

LEVI, ANTHONY, '*La Princesse de Clèves* and the *Querelle des anciens et des modernes*', *Journal of European Studies* 10 (1980), 62–70.

LOUGEE, CAROLYN C., *Le Paradis des femmes: Women, Salons and Social Stratification in Seventeenth-Century France* (Princeton: Princeton University Press, 1976).

LYONS, JOHN D., 'Narrative, Interpretation and Paradox: *La Princesse de Clèves*', *Romanic Review* 72 (1981), 383–400.

—— 'The Dead Center: Desire and Mediation in Lafayette's *Zayde*', *L'Esprit créateur* 23 (Summer 1983), 58–69.

MACLEAN, IAN, *Woman Triumphant. Feminism in French Literature 1610–1652* (Oxford: Clarendon Press, 1977).

MAGENDIE, MAURICE, *La Politesse mondaine et les théories de l'honnêteté en France au XVIIe siècle, de 1600 à 1660* (Paris: Félix Alcan, 1925).

MALANDAIN, PIERRE, 'Ecriture de l'histoire dans *La Princesse de Clèves*', *Littérature* 36 (Dec. 1979), 19–36.

—— *Madame de Lafayette, 'La Princesse de Clèves'* (Paris: Presses Universitaires de France, 1985).

Mercure galant, Le, Apr., July and Oct. 1678 (*Extraordinaire*), and Mar., May and Oct. 1678 (*Ordinaire*).

MILLER, NANCY K., 'Emphasis Added: Plots and Plausibilities in Women's Fiction', *PMLA* 96 (1981), 36–48.

MOULIGNEAU, GENEVIÈVE, *Madame de Lafayette, romancière?* (Brussels: Editions de l'Université de Bruxelles, 1980).

NIDERST, ALAIN, *La Princesse de Clèves de Madame de Lafayette* (Paris: Nizet, 1977).

RAITT, JANET, *Madame de Lafayette and 'La Princesse de Clèves'* (London: Harrap, 1971).

RELYEA, SUZANNE, 'Elle se nomme: la représentation et la lettre dans

La Princesse de Clèves', in *Onze Nouvelles Etudes sur l'image de la femme dans la littérature française du XVIIe siècle*, ed. Wolfgang Leiner (Tübingen: Gunter Narr Verlag, 1984), 109–19.

RONZEAUD, PIERRE, 'La femme au pouvoir ou le monde à l'envers', *Dix-septième siècle* 108 (1975), 9–33.

SCANLAN, TIMOTHY, 'Silence in *La Princesse de Clèves*', *Nottingham French Studies* 19 (Oct. 1980), 1–15.

SCOTT, J. W., 'Criticism and *La Comtesse de Tende*', *Modern Language Review* 50 (Jan. 1955), 15–24.

—— 'Madame de Lafayette: an Interim Selective and Critical Bibliography', *Newsletter of the Society for Seventeenth-Century French Studies* 1 (1979), 3–6.

—— *Madame de Lafayette. A Selective Critical Bibliography* (London: Grant and Cutler, 1974).

SHOWALTER, ENGLISH, *The Evolution of the French Novel, 1641–1782* (Princeton: Princeton University Press, 1972).

STANTON, DOMNA C. 'The Fiction of *préciosité* and the Fear of Women', *Yale French Studies* 62 (1981), 107–34.

TIEFENBRUN, SUSAN W., 'Big Women', *Romanic Review* 69 (1978), 34–47.

—— 'Madame de Lafayette's Theory of Women and Literature', *Papers on French Seventeenth-Century Literature* (Actes de Fordham, 1983), 223–39.

VALINCOUR, J.-B. DE, *Lettres à Madame la Marquise *** sur le sujet de 'La Princesse de Clèves'* (Paris: Mabre-Cramoisy, 1678).

VENESOEN, CONSTANT, *Etudes sur la littérature féminine au XVIIe siècle* (Birmingham Alabama: Summa Publications, 1990).

VIRMAUX, ODETTE, *Les Héroïnes romanesques de Madame de Lafayette* (Paris: Klincksieck, 1981).

INDEX

❖

Aiguillon, duchesse d' 83
Alfonso VI 42
Anne of Austria, Queen 16, 18, 19, 83
anonymity 1–8, 9, 13, 23, 41, 61, 64, 73–4, 79–80, 83–4
Antin, Madame d' 25
Aronson, Nicole 3
Astrée, L' 50
Aulnoy, Madame d' 3

Baillet, Adrien 1, 2, 4
Beasley, Faith E. 9
Beaunier, A. 2, 12
Bédacier, Madame 69
Bernard, Mlle 69
Biet, Christian 65
Bossuet, J.-B. 12
Brantôme, Pierre de Bourdeille, seigneur de 33
Briggs, Robin 30
Brionne, comte de 29
Bussy-Rabutin 6, 55

Chalais, Madame de 15
Champailler, Yvonne 12
Chanlay, M. de 26
Charles I 10
Charles II 10, 18
Charles IX 33, 43
Charnes, Abbé de 65
Choisy, Abbé de 16
communication 51–5, 58–9, 61–3
Condé, Prince de 41, 44
confession 21–2, 31, 38, 61–2, 65, 68, 70, 71, 75–6, 77–80
confinement 25–6, 29, 33, 46–7, 56–7
Conti, prince de 25
Courtin, M. de 26
Cuénin, Micheline 32

Defodon, C. 34
DeJean, Joan 5, 64, 75, 82
disguise 6–7, 9, 10–14, 16, 56–7, 64
Donneau de Visé 65
Dover, Treaty of 10
Duchêne, Roger, 3, 12, 16, 25, 39–40, 42, 65, 82
Dulong, Claude 3

Elisabeth de France 66
Elizabeth I 33
Esther 30
Estrées, Gabrielle d' 20
Estrées, maréchal d' 27

Fénelon, François de Salignac de la Mothe 34
Force, Mlle de la 3
fortune 17–18, 27–8
Fouquet, Nicolas 10, 17, 18, 27
Francillon, Roger 51, 54
Fumaroli, Marc 3, 9

Gaillard, Roger 75
Galerie des peintures, La 6, 41
games 20, 27, 29, 67–9, 74
Genlis, Madame de 11
Grande Mademoiselle (Mlle de Montpensier) 6, 41–3, 44, 49, 50
Guiches, comte de 10, 11, 14, 15, 16, 20, 21

Harcourt, marquis d' 26
Henri II 66
Henri IV 20
Henriette, princess, *see* Madame
Henriette, Queen 9, 10, 12
Henry VIII 66
Herrmann, Claudine 82

Hirsch, Marianne 70
Huet, Pierre-Daniel 1, 2, 50

James II 27, 28, 29
jealousy 13, 20, 37, 54, 58–9

Kibedi Varga A., 69

La Rochefoucauld, François, duc de 1, 2, 4, 6, 50
Lafayette, Angélique de 10, 12, 13, 17
Lafayette, François, comte de 39, 82
Lafayette, François Motier de 12
Lafayette, Louis de 23, 31
Lafayette, Madame de:
  La Comtesse de Tende 1, 31–40, 42, 61, 73
  Histoire de Madame Henriette d'Angleterre 1, 4, 9–23, 24, 28, 30, 48, 61, 72, 83
  Mémoires de la cour de France 1, 9, 11, 18, 23–30, 31, 46, 48, 56, 67
  'Portrait de Madame la marquise de Sévigné' 1, 6–8, 23, 41, 61, 63, 80
  La Princesse de Clèves 1, 2, 5, 6, 31, 57, 61, 64–80
  La Princesse de Montpensier 1, 2, 3, 14, 41–9, 56, 64, 72, 73
  Zaïde 1, 14, 50–63, 73, 74
language 20–2, 26, 52–3, 55–8, 74, 75–8
Laugaa 3, 5, 12, 65
Lauzun, duc de 42
Lemoine, Jean 23
Lescheraine, J.-M. de 2, 6
letters 10, 21, 22, 35, 38, 46, 50, 76–7, 78, 79
Lever, Maurice 3
Longueville, chevalier de 27
Lorraine, chevalier de 82
Louis XIII 12, 13, 17
Louis XIV 9–29 *passim*, 41, 42, 67, 83
Louvois, marquis de 23–4, 27, 28

Maclean, Ian 33, 41, 69, 83
Madame (Princess Henriette) 10–23, 27
Madame la Duchesse 25–6, 29
Magne, Emile 31

Maintenon, Madame de 29, 30
Malandain, Pierre 65, 67
Mancini, Mlle de 15, 17, 18, 19, 20, 27, 72
Marie-Thérèse, Queen 15, 16
  marriage 14, 35, 39–40, 56–7, 65–6, 67–8, 69–70
Marsan, M. de 29
Mazarin, Cardinal 10, 14, 16, 17, 18, 27
Médicis, Catherine de 32, 33, 34–5, 42, 66, 71–3
Ménage, Gilles 2, 34
Mercure galant, Le 5, 65
misunderstanding 16–18, 52–5, 57–60, 73–4
Monsieur (Philippe d'Orléans) 10, 12, 19, 42, 82
Montalais, Mlle de 10, 20, 21
Montespan, Madame de 25, 30
Montgrédien, G. 16
Montpensier, Mlle de, *see* Grande Mademoiselle
Mouligneau, Geneviève 1
Murat, Madame de 3

narrative voice 6–7, 13, 22, 25, 26, 39, 57, 62–3
Niderst, Alain 31, 32, 81

Petrarch 34
Philippe d'Orléans, *see* Monsieur
Pope 25, 26, 27
power 7, 9, 10, 17, 18–23, 28, 43, 46–8, 66, 68–74, 77–8, 81
Puy-Guilhem, M. de 16

Racine, Jean 30
Rapin, Père René 3
Richelieu, Cardinal 17, 83
Roche-Guilhem, Mlle de la 3
Ronzeaud, Pierre 65
Roquelaure, duchesse de 32

Sabatier de Castres, Abbé 51
Savoie, duc de 12
Savoie, duchesse de 12, 82
Scott, J. W. 32

Scudéry, Madeleine de 3
secrecy 7, 21–2, 33, 35, 38, 40, 63, 67, 68, 70–1, 79
Segrais, Jean de 1, 4, 42, 50
Seignelay, M. de 27, 28
Seneville, Madame de 5, 6
Sévigné, Madame de 1, 6, 23, 24, 25, 41, 61, 63, 80, 82
Sigaux, Gilbert 11
silence 2, 9, 38, 45, 49, 60, 61–5, 76–80, 81
Soissons, comtesse de 10, 15, 19, 20
Sorel, Charles 3
Strozzi, Mlle de 32–3, 34–5

Tonnay-Charente, Mlle de 15, 21
Trimouille, Mlle de la 13

Valentinois, duchesse de (Diane de Poitiers) 20, 71–3
Valentinois, Mme de 16, 26
Valincour, J.-B. de 64, 65
Vallière, Louise de la 10, 16, 19, 21
Valois, Mlle de, *see* Savoie, duchesse de
Valois, Marguerite de 20
Vardes, marquis de 10, 11, 14, 32
Velat, Abbé 12
Versailles 24–5, 26, 27
Villedieu, Madame de 3
Villequier, M. de 20

war 10, 14, 18, 24–9, 43–5, 48
William of Orange 28, 29